DEMCO

Portrait of a Decade

The 1950s

NANCE LUI FYSON

B.T. Batsford Ltd, London

Contents

The original idea for the Portrait of a Decade series was conceived by Trevor Fisher.

© Nance Lui Fyson 1990
First published 1990

Typeset by Tek-Art Ltd Kent
and printed and bound
in Great Britain by
MacLehose and Partners Ltd, Portsmouth
for the publishers
B.T. Batsford Ltd
4 Fitzhardinge Street
London W1H 0AH

A CIP catalogue record for this book is available from the British Library

ISBN 0 7134 6070 9

Frontispiece: The very first march of the Campaign for Nuclear Disarmament (CND), in 1958.

Introduction

Looking back, the decade of the 1950s seems relatively quiet compared to the world turmoil of the 1940s and social upheavals of the 1960s. Yet events in the Fifties prepared the way for explosions and changes in later decades. Movements such as black protest, youth rebellion and even the conquest of space were simmering and beginning to boil.

Nuclear technology offered new possibilities, both good and bad. The introduction of the hydrogen bomb and ballistic missiles brought great changes to military strategies. Scientists were also working to develop the peaceful uses of nuclear power. It was 1956 when 70 nations joined to form the International Atomic Energy Association. Britain, America and Russia all began using nuclear power plants and an atomic-powered submarine, *Nautilus*, moved beneath the North Pole.

There were many other developments in science and medicine, such as the new anti-polio vaccine developed by the American scientist J.E. Salk. Evidence was produced that smoking is linked to lung cancer and heart disease, but tobacco companies still disputed the research.

Spaceflight was taken seriously after Soviet scientists managed to put sizeable satellites into orbit in 1957. The American response was a concern to 'catch up' with the Russians and the race to get to the moon had begun. The use of animals in space flight in the late 1950s allowed scientists to judge the responses of living creatures to space conditions. Scientists had also discovered two major areas of radiation surrounding the earth and the far side of the moon had been photographed.

The race for space was just part of the growing competition and conflict between the USSR and USA. As the decade opened, war in Korea developed. Sixteen nations sent armed forces to the area but it was essentially an American war against Communism. US fears about the Communist 'menace' had been growing since the end of the Second World War. American foreign policy was based on containing Communism, and this led to the US setting up military bases in over a dozen countries (including Japan, the Philippines and West Germany).

A Wisconsin senator, Joseph McCarthy, played on American fears about Communism. In the early 1950s his 'witch-hunt' led to accusations of disloyalty against many US citizens – from film stars to politicians.

Meanwhile, protest about discrimination against blacks was growing in America. Since the late 1800s, a Supreme Court ruling had said segregation was legal as long as facilities for whites and non-whites were equal. (In fact, this was rarely the case.) After 1953, desegregation in the government and armed forces prompted callings for more general desegregation laws. President Eisenhower was doubtful about the use of law to bring about equality, but an historic court decision in May 1954 did start a gradual landslide of change. The Court ruled that segregation of public schools was not in keeping with the American Constitution and that schools must integrate 'with all deliberate speed'. States in the Deep South resisted change. In 1957, the governor of Arkansas sent in the National Guard to try and keep Little Rock Central High School for whites only. The school did become integrated, but by late 1960 less than one-eighth of the South's school districts were desegregated.

Non-violent pressure for racial equality was growing. In 1955 the Reverend Martin Luther King led a boycott against segregation on buses. In

The Russian dog Kozyavka is shown ready for her flight into space in 1959.
The use of animals helped scientists prepare for manned space flights. It was during the Fifties that human fantasies about exploring the universe started to become a reality.

An American soldier questions a captured North Korean boy (1950).

Introduction

the years that followed, sit-ins and other tactics were used to desegregate lunch counters and other facilities. 1957 was the year of the first major civil rights law in America in 82 years.

While minorities and some pressure groups protested for a fairer society, the decade was largely a conservative one. Some observers have called college students of the 1950s the 'silent generation'. For most, the aim was simply to get a job and avoid controversy. Popular books of the decade included those with titles like *The Status Seekers* and *The Organization Man*, showing the basic concern to just 'get on'.

In Europe and especially America many enjoyed increasing prosperity, with wider ownership of homes as well as televisions, cars and other consumer goods. Between 1949 and 1957 the amount spent on advertising doubled in the US. Growing numbers of families were moving out of cities into suburbs, but farmers with small and middle-sized farms were just some of those left out of the US boom. The technological revolution in the countryside used more advanced machinery and methods, favouring big farmers.

Important changes were happening in Europe as countries joined together in treaties. In 1951 France and West Germany joined Belgium, Luxembourg, Italy and Holland to create the European Coal and Steel Community. The European Economic Community (EEC) was formed in 1957, with the aim of eliminating all internal tariff barriers, having a common tariff system for outsiders and allowing free flow of capital and labour amongst EEC countries.

'Co-existence' between countries of East and West was a slogan of the 1950s, as America and Western Europe negotiated with the changing Russian leadership. The death of the Russian leader Stalin was important to events. His later years were marked with purges and executions in East European countries as well as more repression in Russia. The three leaders who at first replaced him (Bulganin, Khrushchev and Molotov) began to relax controls. In June of 1953 there was already heavy rioting in East German cities against Soviet policies.

As Europe became more stable in the 1950s, there were sweeping changes in the Middle East and Africa. Egyptian King Farouk's corrupt regime was overthrown in 1952, with Nasser emerging as the new leader. His nationalization of the Universal Suez Canal Company led to the Suez Crisis of 1956. More Middle-East crises followed in Iran and Iraq.

African colonies were pushing for independence, led by the Gold Coast which became the state of Ghana in 1957. A more violent path was followed in Kenya where the Mau Mau uprising led to a state of emergency being declared in 1952. Apartheid took a firm hold in South Africa as restrictions on blacks increased. Anti-colonial feeling was fuelled by major conferences such as the 1955 Asian-African meeting in Indonesia, the 1957 Asian-African People's Solidarity Conference and the 1958 All-African People's Conference in Ghana.

Anti-Communist feeling dominated events in the Americas. In March 1954 the Organization of American States (OAS) adopted a US resolution that Communism was a threat to the security and peace of the hemisphere. But Latin American feeling was also growing against political and economic

'Teenagers' (who emerged as a distinct new social group in the 1950s) are seen here by a juke box enjoying the shocking new music 'rock 'n' roll'.

One 'first' of the decade was the successful conquest of Mount Everest by Edmund Hillary and the Sherpa guide Tensing in 1953. Here they are greeted by reporters at London airport.

Introduction

domination. When US Vice-President Nixon went on a 'good will' tour of the continent in 1958 he was given a hostile response. Fidel Castro came to power in Cuba in 1959 on this anti-US wave.

The Communist takeover of the Chinese mainland at the end of the 1940s led to a huge programme of development. The Chinese borrowed ideas and technology from the Soviets in the early 1950s but a rift (the 'Sino – Soviet' split) grew between Communist China and Russia later in the decade. China's second five-year economic programme, the Great Leap Forward, was launched in 1958.

The arts developed as well over the decade, with writers as varied as J.D. Salinger, Albert Camus and John Osborne. Abstract Expressionism was the main influence in painting and sculpture. Artists like Willem deKooning and Jackson Pollock splashed and daubed in the early 1950s – while Robert Rauschenberg and Jasper Johns tried for a less emotional style towards the end of the decade. They presented ordinary objects – such as beer cans – as being worthy of art. Sculpture used materials such as welded metal bars and twisted wire to create abstract figures. Composers such as John Cage were also experimenting.

The film industry faced the competitive novelty of television which was dominating mass culture in the Fifties. Hollywood tried such new techniques as 3-D movies and Cinerama to draw back audiences. Popular films of the decade ranged from westerns like *High Noon* and dramas like *On the Waterfront* to musicals like *An American in Paris*. A series of 'Road to . . .' films featured stars like Bob Hope and Bing Crosby.

Film star James Dean symbolized the youth rebellion which was part of the Fifties magic. Black leather, motorcycles, denim, rock 'n' roll music and jive dancing marked a new youth culture. King of this revolution was Elvis Presley.

Sports stars set new records and golf was one of several sports becoming more popular because of television. Some sports teams became legends, like the New York Yankees in baseball who reached the World Series final play-offs of top teams every year of the decade except 1954 and 1959.

While the 1950s were tame years in some ways, seeds of conflict and protest were being sown that decade. The aura of boom times, fun, innocence and glamour was mixed with serious concerns. For the first time, ordinary people were questioning technological progress. Would mankind even survive the amazing new weapons of war?

1954: comedian Jack Benny enjoys the considerable charms of Marilyn Monroe, film goddess of the Fifties.

5

Containing Communism

KOREA BORDERS ON CHINA but was ruled by Japan from 1910 to 1945. When Japan lost the Second World War and surrendered in 1945, Korea became occupied by Soviet forces in the north and American forces in the south. The dividing boundary set was the earth's 38th parallel of latitude. In 1948 Russian and American troops left, leaving a Communist government in the north and a government friendly to America in the south. Both governments felt they had the right to rule all of Korea.

In June 1950, North Korean soldiers crossed the 38th parallel for a full-scale invasion of South Korea. Russia and America were far from friendly at this time. The 'Cold War' between them had been growing in the late 1940s and America saw this invasion as a test of their 'containment' policy. President Truman had vowed that the United States would try and stop Communism from spreading. From 1946, this became the main aim of American foreign policy.

America reacts

PRESIDENT TRUMAN reacted by sending American soldiers and war planes to fight for South Korea. His announcement on 27 June included the following:

The attack upon Korea makes it plain beyond all doubt that Communism has passed beyond the use of subversion to conquer independent nations and will now use armed invasion and war. . . . I know that all members of the United Nations will consider carefully the consequences of this latest aggression in Korea in defiance of the UN Charter.

Truman also persuaded the UN (United Nations) Security Council that the UN should defend South Korea as well. Sixteen countries, including Britain, sent troops but 90 per cent of the anti-Communist forces were American. The overall commander was also American, General Douglas MacArthur.

After three months of hard fighting, US and UN forces managed to push back the Communist forces behind the 38th parallel. The US aim then became to unite all of Korea under a government friendly towards America. A report by the UN Commission in September said that the prospects for uniting Korea were 'more and more remote' and that the country faced the serious danger of a 'most barbarous civil war'. It described the 'world-wide antagonism between the Soviet Union and the US' as 'one of the basic factors underlying the present difficulty'.

The Korean War was marked by movements of people – both civilian and military. Here South Korean women and children were fleeing from Communist troops while American troops moved in for battle.

Korea

China becomes involved

COMMUNIST LEADER MAO ZEDONG had won a struggle to rule China in 1949. The US had tried to keep the Communists from also gaining power in China, but had failed. Mao did not want to see all of Korea becoming an American ally. He sent thousands of Chinese soldiers to help the Communist North Koreans. Thus a fiercer war grew in Korea which was really between the US and China. MacArthur wanted to attack China itself but Truman was against the idea, fearing another world war. MacArthur

English soldiers of the Gloucestershire Regiment. More than a dozen countries sent troops to fight in Korea but it was largely an American war against the spread of Communism.

lost his job for publicly criticizing the President's decision.

In May 1953 one description of the fighting recorded:

At the western end of the front, British and Canadian troops fought a three-hour battle on May 3 with 900 Chinese who attacked UN positions between 'Little Gibraltar' and 'The Hook'; after overrunning forward trenches, the enemy were thrown back after hearing fighting in the dark with bayonets, grenades and tommy-guns. On May 28 the 10,000 Chinese troops with powerful artillery support launched a series of fierce attacks along a 20-mile front in the same sector, directed mainly gainst British troops holding 'The Hook' and American and Turkish troops holding the 'Vegas' and 'Elko' hill positions . . . UN aircraft kept up intensive attacks on enemy communications, supply centres etc. . .'

War finally ends

IT WAS JULY 1953 before the Korean War finally ended. The death of the Russian leader Stalin helped end the fighting as he had been encouraging the Chinese to stay in the war. Another helpful factor was that the new American President Eisenhower hinted that he might use atomic weapons if there were not a cease-fire. The cease-fire left Korea much as it had been before the fighting, divided along the 38th parallel. Both sides claimed a victory. The Chinese said it showed that it paid to stand up to America, and America said it showed that Communists should not try to spread their rule by force.

In his broadcast to American people, President Eisenhower said:

We greet with prayers of thanksgiving the news that an armistice was signed an hour ago in Korea. . . . For this nation, the cost of repelling aggression has been high. . . . With sorrow and with solemn gratitude we think of those who were called upon to lay down their lives in that far-off land.

That evening, Eisenhower asked Congress to authorize an initial emergency fund for the rehabilitation of S. Korea's devastated economy.

The extent of the devastation suffered by the people and the economy is staggering. Since the outbreak of war in 1950, one million S. Koreans have been killed. More than 2,500,000 have become homeless refugees.

On 27 July, the Soviet Premier sent a message to the North Korean Premier:

The signing of the armistice has caused deep satisfaction amongst the Soviet people who regard the successful conclusion of the armistice negotiations as a great victory for the heroic Korean people and the valiant Chinese People's Volunteers.

World News

'Super-bomb' confirmed

ON 30 JANUARY 1950 the US first officially confirmed it was considering the production of a hydrogen 'super-bomb'. President Truman's statement said:

It is part of my responsibility as Commander-in-Chief of the armed forces to see to it that our country is able to defend itself against any possible aggressor.

In February, twelve leading atomic scientists issued a statement urging the US government to declare that it would never use the bomb unless it had first been used against the US or her allies.

We believe that no nation has the right to use such a bomb no matter how righteous its cause. This bomb is no longer a weapon of war but a means of exterminating whole populations. New York or any great city of the world would be destroyed by a single hydrogen bomb.

Delhi Pact signed

THE LEADERS OF India and Pakistan (Pandit Nehru and Mr Liaquat Ali Khan) signed an agreement in April on the minorities issue. This 'Delhi Pact' stated:

The governments of India and Pakistan solemnly agree that each shall ensure to the minorities throughout its territory complete equality of citizenship, irrespective of religion, a full sense of security in respect of life, culture, property and personal honour, freedom of movement within each country and freedom of occupation, speech and worship.

The Pact also gave protection to thousands of minorities who were leaving Pakistan to come to India or leaving India to come to Pakistan.

India and Pakistan became separate nations in 1947, with minorities in both countries being mistreated. For example, in January 1950 Moslems in the Indian area of Garanbazar were being assaulted and their property looted or burned. The riots were started by reports of mistreatment of Hindus in some districts of Pakistan. Violent rioting with arson and looting broke out in Calcutta in February, causing many casualties. This led to many Moslems leaving Hindu areas of the city. There was rioting in Pakistan's capital Dacca as well, with attacks on Hindus. India's Prime Minister issued a statement in February expressing concern and appealing to people not to fall prey 'to communal passion and retaliation'.

In August, Pandit Nehru reported on the progress made by the Delhi Pact. He stated that both the Indian and Pakistani governments had appointed Ministers responsible for the agreement. Inquiry commissions had been set up to report on causes of disturbances and to suggest ways of avoiding troubles in the future. The governments had issued instructions to help ease travel for migrants between the two countries and officers were appointed to see that minorities were being treated fairly.

India's Prime Minister Nehru (1889-1964).

Famine in China

A GRAVE FAMINE IN CHINA was reported by Mr Tung Pi-wu, one of the Vice-Premiers in the Chinese Communist Government, in a February speech. He estimated that over seven million refugees were in urgent need of relief. There had been a series of natural disasters and also destruction of flood control systems during the civil war. Emergency supplies were being distributed and there were austerity measures. By April, Peking radio reported that the number of people facing starvation was as high as 16 million.

Atlee wins

CLEMENT ATLEE was re-elected as Prime Minister in the UK General Election on 23 February. It was the closest result for over a century, with Labour winning by an overall majority of only seven.

Clement and Mrs Atlee are shown ready for their election tour for the UK General Election.

New Marriage Law

A NEW MARRIAGE LAW came into effect on 1 May in China. The law forbade the marriage or betrothal of children, fixing the minimum age at 20 for men and 18 for women. Other parts of the law included forbidding polygamy and accepting money for arranging marriages. A statement issued by the Central Committee of the Communist Party claimed that

implementation of the law will emancipate the people, and especially women, from an age-old system and will make possible a new marriage system, new family relations and a new social morality.

No racial tagging

IN NOVEMBER, the American Red Cross announced that blood in its blood banks would no longer be tagged with the race of the donor.

'Loyalty Day' parades

ABOUT FIVE MILLION AMERICANS marched in anti-Communist 'Loyalty Day' parades on 30 April, showing their loyalty to the American way of life.

Milk rationing ends

The UK Ministry of Food announced the end of milk rationing from 15 January. From that date, the public could buy as much milk as it liked. (Wartime milk rationing began in 1941.)

Some UK wartime rationing continued into the early 1950s. In January 1951 the bacon ration was increased from 4 to 5 oz a week per person and the sweet ration went up from 4 to 4½ oz a week. In April there was an increase in the butter ration but a reduction in the bacon ration. In the summer there was an increase in the meat ration and a reduction in the tea ration. (UK food rationing finally ended in 1954.)

Motor vehicles census

A WORLD-WIDE CENSUS recorded that there were nearly 62½ million motor cars and lorries in the world in 1950. About 69 per cent of these were in the USA and less than 5 per cent were in the UK. Britain had fewer than 3 million cars and lorries.

Chadwick swims channel

IN AUGUST, Florence Chadwick, aged 31, swam the English Channel in 73 hours and 28 minutes, setting a new speed record for women.

Florence Chadwick trained for her record Channel swim by swimming in place for as long as seven hours at a stretch. Here a trainer holds a rope around her body to keep the swimmer's body stationary.

Bald Prima Donna produced

EUGENE IONESCO'S play *The Bald Prima Donna* was seen in Paris for the first time in 1950. the Romanian-born playwright was the father of the so-called Theatre of the Absurd. *The Bald Prima Donna* is a good example of this, dramatizing the absurdity of human life. In the play, Mr and Mrs Smith talk in clichés about the trivia of everyday life. The meaninglessness of life is featured in exchanges where every member of a large family is called Bobby Watson. Mr and Mrs Martin enter the stage. They talk as if they are strangers but discover they are both from Manchester, came to London at the same time, live in the same house and sleep in the same bed. They are the parents of the same child. Other aspects of the play emphasizing absurdity include the doorbell which rings to announce no one. At the end of Ionesco's play, the Martins replace the Smiths in their chairs and start speaking the same lines the Smiths spoke at the start.

Best of sport

AN ASSOCIATED PRESS POLL of sportswriters and sportscasters named Babe Ruth and best baseball player of the past 50 years, Johnny Weismuller the best swimmer, Jack Dempsey the best boxer, Jesse Owens the best runner, Bill Tilden the best tennis player.

Modern pentathlon

THE FIVE EVENTS OF THE PENTATHLON are the 100 metres hurdles, shot, high jump, long jump and 200 metres. The European Championship of 1950 saw introduction of the sport, which then became part of the Olympics in 1964.

Russell wins Nobel Prize

BERTRAND RUSSELL (1872-1970) was awarded the 1950 Nobel Prize for literature. Descended from Lord John Russell, the nineteenth-century British Prime Minister, Russell began his career lecturing in mathematics at Cambridge University. He made his reputation as an outstanding philosopher and writer, including popular books about education and sociology. Russell had strong views on morals and politics and was a founder of the Campaign for Nuclear Disarmament (CND) in the 1950s.

Benny is tops

BILLBOARD magazine's annual survey of radio stations named Jack Benny as America's most popular comedian, Bing Crosby as the most popular male singer, Dinah Shore as the most popular female singer and Edward R. Murrow as the best news commentator. Jack Benny once said when accepting an award: 'I don't deserve this, but then I have arthritis and I don't deserve that either'.

The Wall published

JOHN HERSEY'S novel *The Wall* was published in February 1950. It describes life in the Warsaw ghetto during the Second World War.

England enters the World Cup

THE WORLD CUP competition in soccer began in 1930 but it was 1950 before England (the country where the game began) joined.

Bertrand Russell (1872-1970), mathematician, philosopher, writer.

Continuous casting introduced

'CONTINUOUS' OR 'STRAND' casting of steel was first introduced in 1950. With this method, the molten steel is poured into a vertical mould and cooled by jets of water as it falls. Below, the steel is fed on to a horizontal roller-bed where it is cut into slabs of whatever size is needed.

Standard 625 adopted

EUROPEAN broadcasters meeting in 1950 attempted to fix a common picture standard of 625 lines. This was accepted in most countries except for Britain and France – who did not convert until the 1960s and 70s. Nearly all countries now have 625-line television except for the USA, Japan and a few others with the American 525 line system.

First general credit card

THE FIRST CREDIT CARDS for general buying were issued by Diners' Club Incorporated in 1950. From 1954, with the start of a business computer able to control large numbers of formal transactions, credit cards spread widely. By the early 1980s, there were over 300 million cards in the US alone for a population of 220 million people. The growing use of credit cards has been reducing the use of cash.

First mass-produced computer

THE FIRST UNIVACs started coming off the production line in 1950. UNIVAC I (standing for Universal Automatic Computer) was designed and built in Philadelphia, USA.

Smoking linked to lung cancer

TWO REPORTS in the May journal of the American Medical Association revealed that lung cancer was considerably more prevalent amongst heavy smokers than amongst light smokers and non-smokers. In July, delegates to the Fifth International Cancer Conference put out the statement that long-term cigarette smokers seem more susceptible to lung cancer than pipe or cigar users or non-smokers.

Jaws discovered

THE SOUTH AFRICAN anthropologist Robert Broom reported the discovery of two jaws in Northern Transvaal caves which he believed to be those of the last 'missing link' between man and ape.

Californium discovered

UNIVERSITY OF CALIFORNIA scientists discovered a new element, californium, in 1950. It is the heaviest atom known, and is numbered 98 in the periodic table.

Clay tablet found

ARCHEOLOGISTS say they have found a clay tablet recording a 3800 years-old murder trial (the oldest known) in the Iraqi ruins of ancient Nippur.

Radioactive warning

FOUR ATOMIC SCIENTISTS warned that the hydrogen bomb could exterminate the world's population by enveloping the earth in radioactive dust.

In brief . . .

– First human kidney transplant, in Chicago (45-minute operation)
– First gas-turbine automobile (Britain)
– First mechanical onion harvester (USA)
– First concentrated milk, made by Sealtest, sold in Delaware

Reds under

McCarthy witchhunt

US FEARS OF 'Reds under the bed' – Communists invading American life – were rife in the early 1950s. Accusations and denials became part of daily life, fuelled by a Wisconsin Senator Joseph McCarthy. In 1950 he charged in a speech that the State Department (the equivalent of the UK Foreign Office) was full of Communists. He never substantiated his claim but the Senator became the centre of a 'witchhunt' against 'subversive activities'.

Senator McCarthy made wild charges about Communists and their party organization in America. Here he is pointing out the areas of America affected by Communists.

Security Acts

IN SEPTEMBER 1950 Congress overrode President Truman's veto and passed a McCarran Internal Security Act. This established a Subversive Activities Control Board and would not let anyone who had once been a member of a totalitarian organization enter the

America was already in a suspicious mood. Russia's rapid development of the atomic bomb in the late 1940s was thought to be due to secrets being leaked by American traitors. McCarthy exploited this feeling and the early 1950s were marked by investigations of government officials, imposition of loyalty oaths, harassment of scientists and harsh new laws against suspected subversives.

United States. The Act also put tight restrictions on Communist activities and allowed for a 'round-up' of subversives in any national emergency. A second McCarran Act, the Immigration and Nationality Act of 1952 said that foreigners visiting the US must go through complicated loyalty checks.

President Truman was concerned for the effects on individual civil liberties. In January 1951 he appointed a Commission on Internal Security and Individual Rights. This was to study the problem of 'providing for the internal security of the US and at the same time protecting the rights and freedoms of individuals'. Under special consideration was the Government's employee loyalty and security programme. Truman pointed out the danger that measures taken to protect the nation against subversive activities might 'infringe the liberties granted by the Constitution'.

In August 1951, Patrick McCarran, chairman of the Senate Internal Security Subcommittee charged that between three and five million subversive aliens lived in the US and were a threat 'potentially more dangerous than that of an armed force'. The following month, film writer Martin Berkeley testified before the House Un-American Activities Committees, listing over 100 alleged Communists he had known in Hollywood.

Meanwhile, Elenor Roosevelt (wife of the former president Franklin D. Roosevelt) attacked McCarthy as 'the greatest menace to freedom because he smears people without the slightest regard for the facts'.

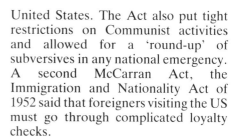

COMMUNIST PARTY ORGANIZATION U.S.A-FEB.9,1950

the Bed

Further investigations

IN NOVEMBER 1951 the Supreme Court warned against the use of 'principles of totalitarianism' in the nation's campaign against Communism. The debate simmered on in 1952. In December, McCarthy announced plans to investigate 'Communist thinkers' and subversive influences in US colleges when he became chairman of the Senate Investigations Subcommittee.

In June 1953, Albert Einstein issued a public letter urging 'every intellectual who is called . . . to refuse to testify'. In August the Senate Internal Security Subcommittee charged that 'the Soviet international organization' had penetrated the US Government 'from the lower ranks to the top-level policy and operating positions' and stolen 'thousands' of secrets due to the Truman Administration's failure to act on FBI reports. The American Bar Association's House of Delegates adopted a report urging action to disbar all lawyers who were Communists.

In September 1953 the House Un-American Activities Committee released the testimony of a former Communist alleging that about 600 Protestant clergy were 'secret [Communist] party members'. The Senate Internal Security Subcommittee charged that US Communists were hiding printing presses and duplicating equipment for underground use in case of war.

McCarthy began a one-week-long speech making tour in February 1954, in which his theme was that: '. . . The Democratic Administration over the past 20 years has deliberately and knowingly allowed Communists to take any position in government they desire'.

Hollywood stars, led by Humphrey Bogart and Lauren Bacall, marched in protest at all the accusations.

McCarthyism condemned

IN JUNE, the McCarthy Investigations Subcommittee ended 35 days of televised hearings on Communist influence in the federal government. In August, a Senate committee considered censure proposals against Senator McCarthy. Then in December the Senate voted 67 to 22 against McCarthy.

Although 'McCarthyism' was increasingly out of favour, the anti-Communist fervour had not slowed entirely. In January 1956 an inquiry was resumed into alleged Communist infiltration of New York City newspapers. The playwright Arthur Miller admitted in June that he had

'erred' in signing appeals by Communist front groups in the 1940s. He agreed to sign an affidavit certifying he was not a Communist. In January 1957, the House Un-American Activities Committee issued a new list of 733 organizations and publications cited as Communist fronts or agencies.

Senator Joseph McCarthy died in May 1957 at the age of 48 from liver failure caused by excessive drinking. The witchhunt became less fervant but some people's careers had already been ruined. The McCarthy era became something which America was not proud to recall in later years.

World News

Peron re-elected

ARGENTINA'S Presidential elections on 11 November resulted in another victory for President Juan Peron. These were the first elections held under a new constitution which allowed re-election of a President and Vice-President. This was also the first election in which women were allowed to vote and be elected.

In August a mass demonstration had called for Peron's wife Señora Eva Peron to accept the nomination for Vice-President. However she announced in a broadcast on 31 August that she had decided not to stand. Her decision may have been due partly to opposition from the Army which objected to the possibility of her acting as Commander-in-Chief in Peron's absence or illness. She was also barely past the minimum age under the constitution for vice-presidential candidates of 30.

President Juan Peron of Argentina and his wife Eva. (She died of cancer in 1952 at the age of 33.)

Iron and steel nationalized

THE UK IRON AND STEEL INDUSTRY was transferred to public ownership on 15 February 1951, 'Vesting Day'. In September 1950 there had been a parliamentary debate and the Conservative Party's opposition to nationalization was defeated. On 7 February 1951 the Conservatives tried again to postpone 'Vesting Day' without success. Mr George Strauss, the Minister of Supply, asserted the Labour Government's view that the steel industry would benefit by removing conflict between the public interest and the interests of private shareholders:

One of the main purposes in nationalizing this great industry is that it should serve the country in peace or war unfettered by any conflicting desire, in the minds of those who run it, to maximize the profits of private shareholders.

Churchill elected

THE GENERAL ELECTION on 25 October resulted in the defeat of Labour and the victory of the Conservative government. Clement Atlee had been elected Labour Prime Minister in 1945 and again in 1950. Winston Churchill, the wartime Prime Minister, again became leader in 1951. In his election broadcast, Clement Atlee noted Britain's position had improved since the Second World War (British exports were 75 per cent higher in 1950 than in 1938). But he admitted that there were still serious shortages:

We have not enough coal and electric power. . . . There is a shortage of houses. We are limited by available supplies and manpower. Years of bad and insufficient housing cannot be remedied quickly.

Festival of Britain

THE FESTIVAL OF BRITAIN was opened formally on 3 May 1951, celebrating 100 years since the Great Exhibition of 1851. King George VI declared the Festival officially open in a speech delivered on the steps of St Paul's Cathedral:

I see this festival as a symbol of Britain's abiding courage and vitality. . . In this Festival we look back with pride and forward with resolution. In celebration of Britain's rich and varied past, we have gathered together not only in London but throughout the land . . . a record of our national character and its history. . . . I have been told of the pageants and displays which have been prepared in our ancient cities and throughout the countryside. . . . Many of these activities and displays will be of lasting value.

Later the same evening, several of the Royal Family attended the official opening of the Royal Festival Hall on the South Bank site in London.

A South Bank Exhibition (open 4 May – 30 September) was the centre-piece of the Festival of Britain. Covering an area of 27 acres (11 ha.), the Exhibition included many pavilions illustrating all aspects of British life and achievement. A prominent feature was the 300-foot (91-metre) high Skylon, a vertical pillar illuminated at night. One main building was the Dome of Discovery, the largest unsupported structure of its kind in the world. The building showed the story of British achievement in fields of scientific research, discovery and exploration. The Land of Britain pavilion used murals, models and films to show climatic conditions, mineral wealth and the physical evolution of Britain over millions of years. The Power and Production Pavilion had a model coalmine and showed craftsmen working textiles, silverware, glass and pottery. The exhibition of Architecture in Poplar, east London, covered a site of 30 acres (12 ha.) and was part of a larger 124-acre (55 ha.) site due to be completely rebuilt under the County of London plan.

The Festival of Britain on London's South Bank site included (left) the Dome of Discovery, the Skylon (pointing high into the sky) and (right) the Transport Pavilion.

Family planning programme

PRIME MINISTER NEHRU OF INDIA reported in July on the recommendations of a special government commission. He urged the start of a birth control programme and India was the first country in the world to have an official campaign for family planning.

Apartheid strengthened

IN MARCH 1951 South Africa's Group Areas Act became effective in Cape Province, Transvaal, Natal and Orange Free State. The Act divided the country on a racial basis, allowing the Interior Ministry to set areas for exclusive ownership or occupation by white, black or coloured people.

Life spans

THE US PUBLIC HEALTH SERVICE reported that the average life span of white American women was a record 71 years compared to 65.5 years for the average white man. For non-whites, the average was 62.5 years for women and 58.1 years for men.

British defectors

TWO SOVIET AGENTS at the Foreign Office, Guy Burgess and Donald Maclean, who had been recruited while students at Cambridge University, were warned in 1951 by H.A.R. (Kim) Philby that their activities were being investigated by the British government. Burgess and Maclean fled to the USSR, and Philby was asked to resign, in view of his Communist associations.

Sport and the Arts

Salinger novel published

J. D. SALINGER'S NOVEL *Catcher in the Rye* was published in 1951. Seventeen-year-old Holden Caulfield is due to be expelled from school for neglecting his studies. He decides not to stay until the end of term but goes instead to a New York hotel. Holden's search for himself and his dislike of 'phonies' in society found favour with the new American youth culture trying to find its way in the 1950s.

I was about half in love with her by the time we sat down. That's the thing about girls. Every time they do something pretty, even if they're not much to look at, or even if they're sort of stupid, you fall half in love with them, and then you never know *where* the hell you are. . . .

Take most people, they're crazy about cars . . . and if they get a brand-new car already they start thinking about trading it in for one that's even newer. I don't even like old cars. I mean they don't even interest me. I'd rather have a god-dam horse. A horse is at least *human*, for God's sake.

Parachuting

PARACHUTING became a recognized sport in 1951, with the staging of the first world championships in Yugoslavia.

Matisse designs

FRENCH ARTIST HENRI MATISSE designed murals, furniture, stained glass and vestments for the Chapel of the Rosary, Vence, France. Matisse once said:

What interests me most is neither still life nor landscape, but the human figure. It is through it that I best succeed in exposing the almost religious feeling I have towards life.

Cycle race

THE TOUR OF BRITAIN was first held in 1951, and became an annual event in 1958 with the title The Milk Race.

Champion boxer Sugar Ray Robinson, who in 1951 won the American middleweight championship twice, having lost it briefly in that year to the British boxer Randy Turpin.

Cage's 'Music for changes'

AMERICAN COMPOSER John Cage introduced 'chance' procedures into his music. 'Music for Changes', first performed in 1951, was determined by tosses of a coin. Cage's innovations gained him an international reputation in the 1950s. His notorious 4'33" (1952) is silent, and consists of whatever environmental sounds can be heard during the 4 minutes and 33 seconds of the piece's duration.

King and I opens

ROGERS AND HAMMERSTEIN'S musical *The King and I* opened on Broadway, featuring Yul Brynner as the King of Siam and Gertrude Lawrence as the English governess who tries to bring Western civilization to his court.

Caine Mutiny published

HERMAN WOUK'S NOVEL *The Caine Mutiny* was published in March of 1951. It tells the story of cruelty and cowardice on a mine-sweeper in the Pacific war. (No real ship like the *USS Caine* existed in World War II.)

. . . Commander Queeg was given command of an obsolete, decaying, run-down ship. He brought it through fifteen months of combat unscathed and a multitude of assignments to the satisfaction of his superiors. There's no complaint against him on the record of his superiors – only by his underlings. . .

Colour TV begins

THE FIRST TRANSMISSION of colour television began in the USA in 1951, using the 'whirling disc' system. The experiment was largely a failure. One problem was that black-and-white sets could not pick up the colour programme, even in monochrome. The few expensive colour sets that were around went blank whenever a programme was broadcast in black and white.

World's first atomic heating plant

SUCCESSFUL TESTS of central heating by atomic energy were made at the Atomic Energy Research Establishment at Harwell near Didcot in Oxfordshire. The Ministry of Supply reported on 17 November that a building at Harwell with 80 offices would from the following day draw its heat directly from the large experimental atom pile. The Ministry said that eventually two or three more buildings would be heated by atomic energy, cutting coal consumption by at least 1000 tons a year.

Cahow found

THE AMERICAN MUSEUM of Natural History in New York reported that the cahow, a sea bird thought to be extinct since the 1620s, had been found alive on small islands off the coast of Bermuda.

Contraceptive pill research

IN THE LATE 1940s a group of chemists and biochemists in Mexico were studying chemicals called steroid hormones. These are vital substances produced in tiny quantities in some human glands. By 1960 this work resulted in the commercial marketing of a simple contraceptive pill. 1951 was an important year marking the start of some key laboratory studies leading to this success.

Steroids are classified into two main groups: sex hormones, controlling the reproductive systems, and adrenocortical steroids, regulating body metabolism. There are three types of sex hormones: androgens (male hormones), oestrogens (female hormones) and progestins. The pregnancy hormone progesterone is the main progestin.

Researchers were trying to find an inexpensive source of steroids to use in controlling reproduction and some diseases. In the late 1940s a way was found of producing progesterone from wild Mexican yams. In 1949 the miracle drug cortisone was first produced from progesterone. Early in 1951, a new progestin called norethindrone was made and a year later a similiar norethynodrel was made. These technological advances led to the production of a birth control pill.

Margaret Sanger was a great campaigner for birth control and the right of women to plan their families. In 1951 she met with Gregory Pincus, a reproduct biologist, and encouraged him and others to try laboratory tests. In 1956 trials on real women began in Puerto Rico. By the end of 1959, studies had shown that norethynodrel was an effective oral contraceptive. The first pills were marketed in 1960.

Margaret Sanger helped promote birth control research in the 1950s which led to the contraceptive pill.

World's oldest man

THE SOVIET HEALTH PUBLICATION *Medical Worker* reported in February that the oldest man in the Soviet Union and probably the whole world was Masmir Kiut, a 154 year old Caucasian peasant.

In brief . . .

– FIRST power steering in cars (USA).

1952 Mau Mau

State of emergency

'ON 26 SEPTEMBER, Mau Mau armed with knives and spears attacked a number of European farms in the Nanyuki area, slaughtered cattle and sheep and burned down a power station. . .' Events like this in 1952 led to Kenya's Governor declaring a state of emergency on 21 October. 'Mau Mau' was a secret black African organization that attacked white farmers, trying to drive them out of the country. The British Colonial Secretary Oliver Lyttelton explained to the British House of Commons:

Since the middle of September the situation has become progressively worse. Once crimes were committed by stealth, but now law and order are challenged in broad daylight. . . . Firearms and gelignite continue to be stolen and firearms instead of knives are being increasingly used by the terrorists.

Terrorists or freedom fighters?

THE MAU MAU belonged to Kenya's largest African group, the Kikuyu tribe, who resented whites owning most of Kenya's best land. A Kikuyu song had the lyrics 'What is misery? It is a man without land.' At the invitation of the Kenyan African Union (KAU), two Labour members of the British Parliament Mr Fenner Brockway and Mr Leslie Hale visited Kenya in late October. Their view of Mau Mau was somewhat different from the Colonial Secretary's:

We disagree profoundly with Mr Lyttelton when he says that social and economic grievances are not the cause of Mau Mau. Mau Mau is an ugly and brutal form of extreme nationalism. It is based on frustration. . . . These frustrations arise from, among other things, the humiliation of the colour bar, the destruction of the old tribal system without the substitution of a satisfactory new system, land hunger, wages which do not in thousands of cases satisfy physical hunger, appalling housing conditions, and the fantastic rise in the price of posho (maize flour), the staple food of the people.

We have been delighted and surprised by the extent of agreement among men and women of goodwill – Europeans, Asians, Africans, and Arabs – as to the measures necessary to meet the situation. Responsible opinion in all four races now accepts the need for the progressive elimination of the colour bar; the extension of co-operative farming in African reserves. . .; the reduction in the price of posho by a subsidy or other method; the advance in wage standards; the rapid improvement in housing conditions; extension of free education; and democratization of the local administration.

We have heard it suggested that the Kenya African Union should be proscribed [outlawed]. This would be a disastrous mistake. It would intensify bitterness and spread a feeling among Africans that the Government is using the crimes of the Mau Mau to strike at legitimate African rights. . . . If the KAU were dissolved by Government action the Africans would lose the right to express themselves through their own most representative organization. . .

A young Kikuyu woman.

Uprising

Programme for change

A PROGRAMME for the economic and social development of Kenya was announced by the British government in late October. Besides rounding up the Mau Mau, the Colonial government also decided it must try to improve conditions to combat unrest. Plans included the construction of new hospitals and health centres, more housing, planting of trees, more welfare activities such as community centres and village halls. Mau Mau activists had jolted an awareness that black Africans wanted real change.

British troops struggled with the Mau Mau for four years and fighters were either killed or put in prison camps. By 1956 over 11,000 Mau Mau had been killed and some 20,000 were in detention. The explosion of Mau Mau had marked the end of white rule in Kenya and steps were taken to lead to independence.

Kikuyu men suspected of being part of Mau Mau were questioned and many were sent to labour camps.

Jomo Kenyatta

JOMO KENYATTA was one of the main Kikuyu leaders. He denied being part of Mau Mau but was one of those put in prison by the British. He was later released in 1963 and went on to become Kenya's first President when it became independent in 1963. Kenyatta was orphaned at an early age and went to a mission school. He later worked as a carpenter in Nairobi and became President of the Kikuyu Central Association. In 1929 he visited Britain to put forward Kikuyu grievances about land. In 1931 he returned to England for a much longer stay of 13 years. Some of this time was spent studying at the University of London. He became the first President of the Pan-African Federation which tried to co-ordinate Black African organizations.

'Winds of Change'

IN THE 1950s, Africa was still very much in the hands of colonial powers. Some countries did gain independence in the decade: Libya became independent in 1951, Sudan, Morocco and Tunisia in 1956, Ghana in 1957, Guinea in 1958. A much larger burst of independence came in 1960 and the 1960s. It was movements such as Mau Mau in the 1950s which showed the frustration of Black Africans and which paved the way.

World News

Rights of women

IN MARCH 1952 a UN Commission on the Status of Women approved a draft convention giving women equal political rights with men throughout the world. The UN General Assembly adopted in December an International Convention on the Political Rights of Women. This guaranteed women the right to vote and hold public office on equal terms with men. (A UN survey at the start of the 1950s showed that women had full political equality in 52 countries but lacked it in 22 countries and were not permitted to hold public office in 12, including Switzerland.)

Struggle over South Africa

THE UN GENERAL ASSEMBLY'S Special Political Committee recommended in January that South Africa's segregation laws be suspended. In June, non-whites in South Africa began a non-violent campaign against the country's racial segregation laws. In November there were three days of race riots with 22 deaths. The African National Council appealed for non-violence, in keeping with its passive resistance campaign against the government's racial policies.

Indonesia in Colombo plan

IN DECEMBER 1952 Indonesia announced it would be part of the Colombo Plan. The six-year Colombo Plan for Co-operative Economic Development in South and South-East Asia was inaugurated in 1951. The region covered included India, Pakistan, Ceylon (now Sri Lanka), the Federation of Malaysia, Singapore, North Borneo, Sarawak, Brunei, Thailand and Indo-China. Nearly a quarter of the world's people were living in those areas but natural wealth was not keeping up with population growth. There was great poverty amongst millions of people.

The Second World War had brought heavy losses to southern south-east Asia. Combined with the post-war world shortage of shipping, this caused hardship to production and transport of foodstuffs and raw materials in the area. The Colombo Plan involved British, Canadian, Australian and New Zealand assistance to help development in the region. Some of the main projects of the plan included new irrigation schemes, development of ports, new hydro-electric schemes and new factories for products like cement and plywood.

Immigration to US and Britain

A NEW CONTROVERSIAL Immigration law in 1952 affected immigration to both America and Britain. For some years West Indians had been leaving their islands looking for work, but they had gone mainly to the US and Central America. The US Immigration Act of 1952 temporarily halted West Indian immigration there and Britain became a main alternative destination.

The years just after the Second World War had stimulated migration to Europe as there were labour shortages. People in the colonies were encouraged to come to Britain to work. The British Nationality Act of 1948 declared Commonwealth citizens as British passport holders, with the right to come to Britain to live. As Britain's economy expanded in the 1950s, there was a shortage of labour so migrants from the West Indies, India, Pakistan and other places came to fill the jobs. Immigrants put up with low pay, long hours and shift work. In 1953 the number of black immigrants was about 3000 a year. By 1957 it was nearly 47,000. London Transport had opened a recruiting office in Barbados in 1956 and the National Health Service and the Hotels and Restaurants Association followed this lead.

Black immigrants in the 1950s faced harsh discrimination in housing and jobs. Notices saying 'NO COLOUREDS' were familiar outside rented housing and other places. Ajit Singh Rai was one immigrant who came to Britain from India in 1956. He had a university degree and expected to find a job according to his qualifications. 'But if I could get a job it was a night job and the dirtiest job. The whole lot of us that come to this country had to live with the very crudest type of discrimination. We were offered only the lowest paid jobs.' As early as 1950, a Bill to try and outlaw racial discrimination in Britain was introduced in Parliament but it was not until the middle of the 1960s that

King Farouk abdicates

King Farouk of Egypt last night sailed out of Alexandria Harbour in the Royal Yacht – a king no longer. He was on his way to exile . . . after being forced to abdicate by Field Marshal Neguib . . .
The People, 27 July 1952.

King Farouk had come to the throne at the age of 16 in 1936 but extravagance and corruption led to his downfall. The rift between him and the army grew when it was realized that defective weapons were supplied for the Palestine war. Farouk protected

entourage who profited from the faulty arms.

When Farouk landed in exile in Italy, he was interviewed by reporters and said:

. . . I wish good luck to those who have taken into their hands and on their consciences the task of governing Egypt. I wish them good luck because they will need it. I hope they will not think that to govern a country in these difficult days of world crises is so easy a task as, perhaps, those who are new to the game may believe.

the first Race Relations Act was passed in Britain.

The total immigration of black people from Asia, Africa and Latin America was not large but it began to worry some people in Britain. Conflicts such as the Nottingham and Notting Hill riots in 1958 reflected tension over race. In 1960 the automatic right of free entry for New Commonwealth citizens was taken away and other restricting Commonwealth Immigration Acts followed.

This Illingworth cartoon appeared in 1953 showing the dense and lethal mixture of fog and industrial smoke which settled on London in December 1952. A Beaver Committee was sent to report on London's serious problem of air pollution.

Immigrants from the West Indies and Indian sub-continent came to Britain in their thousands in the 1950s. Britain still needed more workers and encouraged the immigration.

Sport and the Arts

'Singing in the Rain' starring dancer Gene Kelly was one of many stylish musical films of the decade.

The Old Man and the Sea

ERNEST HEMINGWAY'S SHORT NOVEL *The Old Man and the Sea* was published in New York and is regarded as his best long short story. The book opens with the following description of the main character:

. . . He was an old man who fished alone in a skiff in the Gulf Stream and he had gone eighty-four days now without taking a fish. Everything about him was old except his eyes and they were the same colour as the sea and were cheerful and undefeated.

East of Eden

JOHN STEINBECK'S *East of Eden* was published in 1952 and became one of the year's best-selling novels. The story is about the interaction of the Trask and Hamilton families in what was John Steinbeck's own home valley. He originally began the book as a history of his own family. More generally, *East of Eden* presents American life as it was during the half-century between the Civil War and the start of the First World War. From Chapter 13:

. . . Sometimes a kind of glory lights up the mind of a man. It happens to nearly every one. You can feel it growing or preparing like a fuse burning towards dynamite. . . . The skin tastes the air, and every deep-drawn breath is sweet. . . . This I believe: that the free, exploring mind of the individual human is the most vital thing in the world. And this I would fight for: the freedom of the mind to take any direction it wishes, undirected. . .

The African Queen

HUMPHREY BOGART received an Oscar award for his performance in the film *The African Queen*. The story is set in 1915 when a hard-bitten, gin-drinking river trader (Bogart) and a prim missionary spinster (Katherine Hepburn) make strange companions on a boat down a dangerous African river. Producer Sam Spiegal was one of the first producers to have his stars working on real African locations.

Piaf marries

FRENCH SINGER EDITH PIAF married singer Jacques Peals in 1952. Piaf (1915-1963) was the daughter of an acrobat and had a difficult, unhappy childhood. At an early age she was singing on the streets to support herself but once she began her career in cabaret, Piaf became immensely popular. She wrote both words and music for 'La Vie en rose' which became one of her best-known songs.

High Noon

NEW YORK FILM CRITICS named *High Noon* as the best film of 1952. Gary Cooper was the Western hero, the marshall who received no help when he determined to defend his town against revengeful badmen. *Life* magazine said of the film: 'Few recent Westerns have gotten so much tension and excitement into the classic struggle between good and evil.'

Limelight

CHARLES CHAPLIN'S last major film *Limelight* was released in 1952. In this sentimental film a broken-down music hall comedian is encouraged by a young ballerina to a final triumphant hour.

Hydrogen bomb explodes

THE UNITED STATES successfully tested the first hydrogen bomb in 1952. Its explosive power came from the fusion or combining of the two atomic nuclei of two isotopes of hydrogen, called deuterium and tritium. This process of fusion is like that used by the sun itself to produce energy. In order for the fusion to start, temperatures like that of the sun need to be achieved by exploding an atom bomb within the hydrogen bomb casing. The fusion causes a huge explosion and also sends out neutrons into a layer of uranium, splitting the uranium atoms. More energy is thus released, as well as large quantities of radioactive fission products which spread across the earth as fallout in later years.

The force of a hydrogen bomb can be up to 3000 times more than the atom bomb exploded at Hiroshima in 1945. A hydrogen bomb explosion causes a fire-ball about 3½ miles (approx. 6.5 km) wide, with complete destruction within a radius of 3½ miles (approx. 6.5 km) from the centre. Such a bomb would also cause heavy damage up to 5 miles (8 km) away, moderate damage up to 15 miles (24 km) from the centre and light damage up to 25 miles (40 km) away.

First heart-pacemaker

IN 1952 DR PAUL M. ZOLL of the Harvard Medical School used an electric pacemaker on a 72-year-old man. When the heart's own ability to keep beating regularly is impaired, a low and irregular beat may be the result. A pacemaker implanted under the skin of the abdomen stimulates the heart with minute electric shocks. (By the early 1980s, over a third of a million people worldwide were using pacemakers.)

Cinemascope

A NEW EXPERIENCE FOR CINEMA AUDIENCES appeared in 1952. 'Cinemascope' was started, offering an extra wide-screen system. The key was making films using an expensive anamorphic lens which makes an image half its normal width. When the film is projected, the lens works in reverse and increases the image to twice the traditional screen width. The audience is surrounded by sound as well as image, with loudspeakers around the auditorium.

Other wide-screen systems were tried as well, such as Todd-AO. 'Cinerama' at first used three synchronized projectors giving a curved picture of 146 degrees, approximately the same curvature as the human eye. Later only one projector was used. Todd-AO used one projector with 70mm film. These two systems both make use of six magnetic sound tracks and curved screens.

Cinerama, introduced in 1952, used three synchronized projectors. They gave a curved picture of 146 degrees – about the lateral visual range of the human eye. A fourth film carried sound tracks that were broadcast through loudspeakers around the cinema.

In brief . . .

– first commercial jet service (Britain)
– first transistor hearing aid (USA)
– first tranquillizer marketed (USA)
– Britain exploded its first atomic weapon in a secret test off the north-west coast of Australia.
– The 1951 national UK census showed that one household in 20 still had no piped water. One household in three still did not have a plumbed in bath.

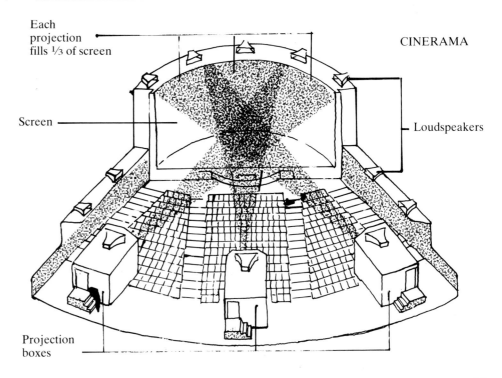

Each projection fills ⅓ of screen

CINERAMA

Screen

Loudspeakers

Projection boxes

Death of

Sharansky remembers

ANATOLY SHARANSKY remembers very well when the Russian leader died:

I was only five when Stalin died, but the memory of that day in 1953 is still clear in my mind. Solemn music filled the streets from radio loudspeakers and the people of Stalino, as the Ukranian city of Donestsk was known in those days, wore black armbands.

To me Stalin was merely a symbol, a word from a verse we repeated like an oath in kindergarten: 'Thank you Comrade Stalin, for our happy childhood.'

My father was a journalist who wanted us to learn the facts from him, rather than in the streets. He told us that Stalin had killed many innocent people, that in his final years he had begun persecuting Jews, and we were very fortunate this terrible butcher was dead. Then he warned us not to repeat these comments to anyone.

Stalin's reign

JOSEPH STALIN WAS BORN IN 1879, the son of a cobbler and washerwoman in a village in Georgia. By 1899 he had joined the political underground and took part in the October Revolution of 1917 which brought Communism to Russia. When the Russian leader Lenin died in 1924, Stalin was one of three men assuming power. By 1928 he alone had gained control of the Communist Party and Russia.

Lenin had let peasants hold on to land they had taken in the Revolution and many were making a good living. In 1929 Stalin began forcing peasants to give up their separate farms. Land and animals were being pooled into large new farms called collectives. Stalin thought this would increase production and allow for better use of machines like combine harvesters and tractors. Millions of landholding peasants called 'kulaks' resisted the change to big collective farms. Stalin ordered soldiers and workers into the country to take foodstuffs from these peasants who then reacted by burning crops and killing animals. Stalin was savage and deported some five million of the resisting peasants to slave labour camps (*gulags*) in Siberia. Millions more people died of starvation or disease or were killed by secret police.

The first collective farms did not work well. Many peasants sent to prison camps were some of the nation's best farmers. Output of main crops like wheat fell and famine swept the countryside in 1932–3. Over five million people starved on some of the world's best farmland. Stalin changed his plans, allowing many peasants to

Marshall Joseph Stalin (1879-1953) ruled Russia with a reign of terror.

Stalin

return to villages. They were given small private plots of land to encourage hard work but it was not until 1954 that farming output again reached the output of 1929.

Stalin's plans also included rapid industrialization. There were projects to build steel mills and to drill oil wells. By 1935 there had been a great increase in industrial production. The Communist Party presented Stalin as a genius and anyone objecting was sent to slave labour camps. Great purges of killing began in 1934 with top generals, politicians as well as ordinary people among the victims. In 1940 Leon

Khrushchev takes over

WHEN STALIN DIED IN 1953, there was relief amongst other politicians. Russia was then led collectively until 1954 when Nikita Khrushchev took over. He denounced Stalin in 1956 (see p. 45) and tried to 'de-Stalinize' the USSR. Stalin's statues and pictures were removed from public places. The powers of the secret police were

Trotsky was assassinated as another victim of Stalin's ruthless regime. Trotsky was a potential leader of Russia after Lenin and Stalin continued to see him as a threat.

reduced and Khrushchev closed the worst of the prison camps.

Some artists and writers began expressing their real feelings about the Stalin years. Alexander Solzhenitsyn, who had spent years as a *zek* (prisoner) in a labour camp, wrote a novel *One Day in the Life of Ivan Denisovich* telling about life in the camps.

Khrushchev also tried to improve everyday living standards. He said: 'We must help people to eat well, dress well and live well. If after 40 years of Communism a person cannot have a glass of milk or a pair of shoes, he will not believe that Communism is a good thing, no matter what you tell him.' Khrushchev increased wages and saw there were more consumer goods to buy. New blocks of flats were built in cities. However, food was still in short supply in the 1950s, with Russian farmers producing barely enough to feed the population. Khrushchev tried paying farmers more for what they produced on collective farms. In 1958 he began allowing them to keep all they produced on private plots – either to feed their families or to sell.

Despite these changes, there were still many problems and the biggest farming failure was Khrushchev's 'virgin lands' scheme. This included millions of hectares of rolling grasslands in the east of USSR. The land had not been used for crops but Khrushchev decided to encourage the planting of wheat. In 1964, Khrushchev was made to resign. The unsuccessful farming schemes were only part of the reason. Some other Russian leaders didn't like other policies Khrushchev had introduced and also felt de-Stalinization was undermining a belief in Communism.

Russians in the mid-1950s queued in Red Square to visit the tomb of Lenin and Stalin. Shortages of food and goods meant that queuing was a common sight.

World News

Queen Elizabeth II waved to the crowds from the balcony of Buckingham Palace after her coronation.

Coronation of Elizabeth II

HUNDREDS OF THOUSANDS OF PEOPLE thronged the streets of London to cheer the procession between Westminster Abbey and Buckingham Palace. It was a wet June and many people were soaked from waiting overnight. 'Splendour in Abbey Seen by Millions' was the headline in the *Daily Telegraph*. Besides the 8000 people in Westminster Abbey, the coronation was seen by millions on television.

After being crowned on 2 June 1953, Queen Elizabeth II stood on the palace balcony to wave to the crowds. With her were Prince Philip and the young Prince Charles and Princess Anne. There was dancing and singing in the streets on Coronation Night, with much celebrating in homes and pubs as well. Britain had just ended most food rationing, which was necessary because of shortages during and after the Second World War. Everyone hoped the new Elizabethan Age would be brighter.

In her first Christmas broadcast that December, the Queen said: '. . . we must keep alive that courageous spirit of adventure that is the finest quality of youth . . . let us set out to build a truer knowledge of ourselves and our fellow men, to work for tolerance and understanding among the nations, and to use the tremendous forces of science and learning for the betterment of man's lot upon this earth. . .'

Everest is conquered

THE HIGHEST MOUNTAIN in the world is Mount Everest, in the Himalayas on the border between Nepal and Tibet. Everest is over 8800m high. In 1953 the Royal Geographical Society and the Alpine Club sponsored an expedition led by Colonel John Hunt. The team followed a route not tried before and by 29 May the summit was reached by New Zealander Edmund Hillary and a Sherpa guide Tensing.

On 5 June Hillary described how he and Tensing made the final ascent to the summit: 'It was a beautiful day with a moderate wind. As we got there, my companion threw his arms around me and embraced me. I took photographs of Tensing holding a string of flags – those of the United Nations, Britain, Nepal and India.' On 16 June the new Queen Elizabeth II conferred knighthoods on Colonel Hunt and Mr Hillary and the George Medal on Tensing.

US Department created

IN MARCH THE US CONGRESS approved establishing a new Department of Health, Education and Welfare. This grew out of a report by a Commission set up by President Truman in 1951 to investigate the health needs of the nation. The Commission pointed out that the US was 'just about alone among civilised nations in having no adequate departmental representation of the public interest in health.' (President Truman had tried to set up such a department in 1949 and 1950 but Congress had rejected his proposals both times.)

Other recommendations of the report included extending prepayment 'insurance' schemes for personal medical treatment. At that time over half of the US population had some health insurance for hospital care. The President of the American Medical Association objected to the idea that the Federal Government should put in funds for the medical care of a large part of the population. '. . . We find it extraordinary that this commission should recommend a governmental system of paying for medical care which has been rejected repeatedly by the American people, by Congress and by the medical profession.'

Rosenbergs executed

JULIUS AND ETHEL ROSENBERG were accused in America of passing atomic secrets to the Soviet Union. They were executed at Sing Sing Prison, New York on 19 June 1953 after various appeals failed. The Rosenbergs claimed they were innocent and protests on their behalf came from many countries. Religious organizations as well as leading lawyers, politicians and scientists spoke out on their behalf. Thousands of petitions were received at the US Embassy in Paris, as feeling was very strong in France. President Eisenhower said he was satisfied that the 'two individuals have been accorded their full measure of justice'.

Eisenhower as President

THE NOVEMBER 1952 ELECTION brought Dwight D. Eisenhower as the new President of the United States, with Richard Nixon as his Vice-President. Eisenhower was a general who had led the Allied armies in the invasion to rescue Europe in 1944. He began his first term of office in January 1953, saying to the nation:

. . . **We shall be guided by certain fixed principles. . . . . We hold it to be the first task of statesmanship to develop the strength that will deter the forces of aggression and promote the conditions of peace . . . we shall never try to placate an aggressor by the false and wicked bargain of trading honour for security . . . we shall strive to foster everywhere policies that encourage productivity and profitable trade, for the impoverishment of any single people in the world means danger to the well-being of all other peoples . . . we reject any insinuation that one race or another, one people or another, is in any sense inferior or expendable.**

Dwight D. Eisenhower salutes his audience.

IPPF formed

THE FOURTH International Conference on Planned Parenthood meeting in Stockholm established an International Federation of Planned Parenthood. This was headed by Margaret Sanger, founder of the Birth Control Movement in the USA.

Road transport nationalized

IN MAY the British road transport industry was nationalized but the iron and steel industries returned to private ownership.

Sweet rationing ends

THE UK MINISTER OF FOOD told the House of Commons on 4 February that the rationing or price control of chocolate and 'sugar confectionery' would end at midnight. It was pointed out that the end of rationing on sweets would allow the Ministry to reduce its staff by 500 people. Rationing of sweets began in June 1942 and was in force over 10½ years with the exception of four months in 1949. (The Government then tried to de-ration sweets but demand was so heavy that rationing was needed again.)

Sport and the Arts

The Crucible opens on Broadway

AMERICAN PLAYWRIGHT Arthur Miller's drama about Salem witch hunts in 1692 opened to rave reviews. The play invited very obvious comparison between the witch trials of the seventeenth century and the hysteria about Communists in America in the early 1950s. Miller himself had been under investigation for supposed Communist leanings and felt all the anguish of being 'accused'.

In the play, the daughter of a minister falls mysteriously ill. Rumours of witchcraft spread as the girl has been secretly engaged in forbidden dancing in the woods with young friends. When Abigail Williams is accused of wrongdoing, she turns the situation into a plea for help. She says her soul has been bewitched. She tries to get rid of Elizabeth Proctor, wife of an upstanding farmer whom Abigail has once seduced. Led by Abigail, the young girls deflect charges from themselves by accusations against various innocent townspeople whom they dislike.

Goons

RADIO COMEDY THRIVED, with 'The Goon Show' a weekly favourite in the UK. Harry Secombe, Peter Sellers and Spike Milligan used unusual noises to create odd characters such as Major Bloodnok, Eccles and Bluebottle. The humour was nonsensical and drew a cult following.

The musical play The King and I *opened at London's Drury Lane Theatre in October 1953 to huge applause. (The play was first performed in 1951, in the USA.) Valerie Hobson played an English governess who went to work for the Royal Family of Siam. A romance develops between her and the King (Herbert Lom). The cost of a programme at the theatre was sixpence.*

Zorba is published

NIKOS KAZANTZAKIS' novel *Zorba the Greek* was published in New York. It is the story of a passionate old man, Zorba, who feels a conflict between earthly pleasures and his higher spirit ('. . . how simple and frugal a thing is happiness; a glass of wine, a roast chestnut, the sound of the sea. . .'). Kazantzakis considered the double nature of man in many of his writings. 'Struggle' is an important part of life and heroic action is to be admired. As a boy growing up in Crete, Kazantzakis saw the Cretan revolt against the Turks in 1897.

Another character in the book is old Madame Hortense. Her fond memory is of being young and beautiful in 1897. She was wined and dined by all four foreign admirals of the fleets at anchor in Suda Bay. Madame Hortense teased the admirals and pleaded with them to treat the Cretans well. When she was finally rowed ashore, the admirals gave her a salute of canon fire.

Kazantzakis' tombstone was inscribed with his words: 'I believe in nothing, I hope for nothing, I am free . . .' but the Greek Orthodox Church did not allow this inscription to stay.

Baldwin's first novel

BLACK AMERICAN novelist James Baldwin was born in Harlem, New York in 1924. For a short while he followed his father's profession and worked as a preacher. Baldwin's first novel *Go Tell it on the Mountain* appeared in 1953, telling about a day in the lives of members of a Harlem church and, through flashbacks, about their forebears. The book was widely praised for giving insights into black life in America. His second novel, *Giovanni's Room*, appeared in 1956. This was set in Paris, Baldwin's new home.

First heart-lung machine

THE HEART must be stopped for 30 minutes or more during several major types of surgical operation. While the heart is stopped, a heart-lung machine takes over the job of the heart by circulating the blood around the body. The machine also does the job of the lungs by supplying fresh oxygen to the blood. It was in 1953 that an American surgeon carried out the first human heart operation using such a machine.

Electronic firsts

THE ELECTRONIC COMPUTER JAINCOM P-C was developed in Maryland, USA. It was capable of adding two 24-digit figures in an eight-millionth of a second, rechecking its accuracy every 3.2 seconds and exercising 'intelligence of a rudimentary sort'.

Another first was America's fully electronic colour television. This was able to accommodate a colour television signal on the same transmission channel as had served for black-and-white.

DNA structure revealed

TWO BIOLOGISTS working at Cambridge University, the American James Watson and the Englishman Francis Crick revealed the detailed structure of DNA (deoxyribose nucleic acid). This is the long chain-like compound forming the body's genes. Genes hold instructions for growth and control the function of each body cell. Crick and Watson's work was an important milestone in understanding all genetics, and forms the basis for continuing research.

Meat substitute patented

ROBERT BOYER, an American chemist, had been busy in the late 1930s looking for a material other than leather that could be used for car-seat covers. In his research, Boyer discovered that the solid, protein-rich remains of soya beans could be spun into strands, after the oil had been extracted to make margarine. Boyer had the idea that these strands could be made into a bland-tasting substitute for meat. It was 1953 before Boyer finally patented this idea.

In making meat substitutes, the soya solids are first made into a fine flour. This is mixed with binding fluids until the mixture is sticky. The substance is then spun on spinnerets like those which are used to produce nylon fibre. A bath of acids and salts is used to set the fibre. Artificial flavourings are then used and the soya is wound into chunks which can be sliced, minced or granulated. Since the 1960s, textured vegetable protein (TVP) made mainly from soya beans has been available to the public in supermarkets and health-food shops.

Organ transplants possible

IN 1953 A SURGEON IN BOSTON, John P. Merrill, discovered that a twin could give a kidney to his twin without the organ being 'rejected'. (It was years later before drugs were developed to stop rejection in transplants between unrelated people.)

Piltdown man 'hoax'

A MOST ELABORATE and carefully prepared hoax.' This was the startling announcement from Britain's Natural History Museum in 1953 regarding the Piltdown Man skull found in England in 1912. It had been thought that the skull was that of a very early human, about 500,000 years old.

A new model clock radio. Clock faces were used – not digital numbers.

1954 Indo-China

French Indo-China

FRANCE'S EMPIRE in the Far East was well established by the end of the nineteenth century. The area was known as Indo-China and it remained under French control until 1941. Japan then occupied the area during the Second World War but the Indo-Chinese led by the Communist Ho Chi Minh resisted this occupation. By the end of the war the Indo-Chinese people had learned much about resistance and wanted national independence.

France hoped to regain its territory in 1945 but the Indo-Chinese (also called the Vietnamese) did not want to remain a colony. The movement worldwide was for independence. Ho Chi Minh set up a Communist Democratic Republic of North Vietnam but France refused to recognize the nation. Battles took place between the French Army and North Vietnamese soldiers (known as the Vietminh). While the French soldiers looked to fight set battles, the Vietminh used other tactics. They attacked by night and dispersed if threatened by a French advance. Local villagers gave much food and support to the Vietminh.

Dien Bien Phu

FRENCH FORCES occupied the town of Dien Bien Phu in 1954, in the hopes of beating the Vietnamese in a battle. The Vietminh surprised the French with unconventional tactics and surrounded the town with thousands of men. The French Union fortress fell to the Vietminh forces on 7 May after an eight-week siege, the heaviest of the war. As the French army was overwhelmed, the French General de Castries sent out a telephone message: '. . . The situation is extremely grave. Confused fighting everywhere. I feel the end is near. But we will fight to the end. We will destroy our guns and all our radio material. I am blowing up all our installations. The munitions dump is exploding already. . .' Five minutes later the call continued: 'They are a few yards away. . . They have broken through everywhere.'

The fall of Dien Bien Phu marked the end of the French empire in Indo-China. 'Defeat – and Paris Weeps' read the *News Chronicle* headline. 'Dien overrun after 55 days'. There was much grief in France and all State theatres were closed on 7 May. Television was cancelled and radios played only solemn music.

Geneva peace conference

THE GENEVA CONFERENCE on Far Eastern Problems which had started in April continued until July. What had been the old French Indo-China became divided into four territories. North Vietnam was Communist, South Vietnam was non-Communist while Cambodia and Laos were neutral.

There was a plan to hold free elections to later unify the two Vietnams. While about equal in populations, the two Vietnams were somewhat different geographically. The main agricultural areas producing rice, rubber and tea were in South Vietnam. The main industrial areas were in North Vietnam. People living in the North depended heavily on buying their rice from the south.

Anthony Eden, Britain's Foreign Minister at the time spoke at the Geneva Conference:

. . .The agreements concluded today could not in the nature of things give complete satisfaction to everyone. But they have made it possible to stop a war which has lasted for eight years and has brought suffering and hardship to millions of people. They have also, we hope, reduced international tension at a point of instant danger to world peace. These results are surely worth our many weeks of toil. In order to bring about a cease-fire we have drawn up a series of agreements. They are the best that our hands could devise. All will now depend upon the spirit in which those agreements are observed and carried out.

US Secretary of State Dulles made the following statement:

. . .The important thing from now on is not to mourn the past but to seize the future opportunity to prevent the loss of Northern Vietnam from leading to the extension of Communism throughout S.E. Asia and the S.W. Pacific. . . The evolution from colonialism to national independence is thus about to be completed in Indo-China and the free Governments of this area should from now on be able to enlist the loyalty of their people to maintain their independence against Communist colonialism.

Divided

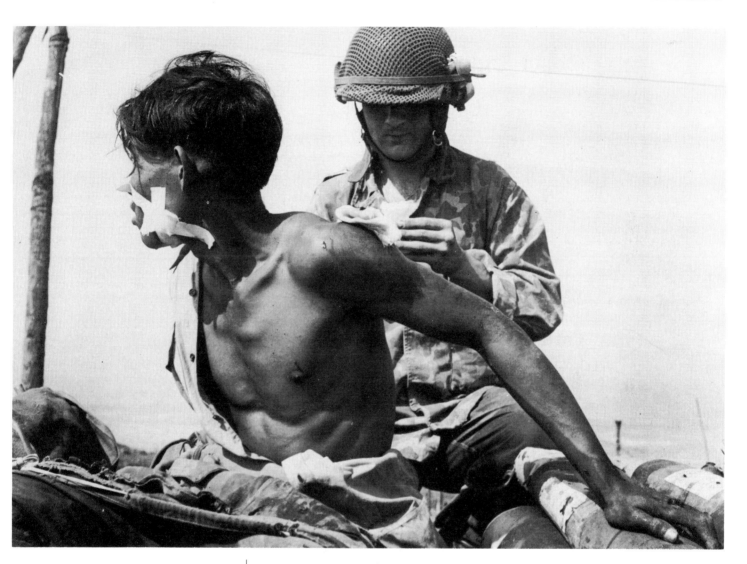

A French soldier helps a wounded Vietnamese colleague who was hurt in the fighting around Dien Bien Phu.

American involvement

PEACE DID NOT LAST LONG IN VIETNAM. Fighting continued in South Vietnam between government forces and Communist guerrillas called Vietcong. Both sides wanted control of the country. America stepped in because it wanted to stop the spread of Communism in the Far East. The US sent in military advisers to help the anti-Communist government and this involvement increased considerably in the 1960s. By the mid-1960s, American bombers were launching heavy raids on North Vietnam and many US troops were there as well. It was the early 1970s before America finally pulled out of Vietnam. The war was very unpopular with many people who felt that America should not have become involved.

Britain signs ESC Treaty

IN DECEMBER, Britain signed a treaty with the European Coal and Steel Community. This established a permanent council of association to co-ordinate community policies in the production and sale of coal and steel.

The European Coal and Steel Community (ECSC) came into being on 25 July, 1952. M. Monnet, President of the High Authority, said of its objectives:

. . . In a few months all Customs barriers, all quantitative restrictions and all discrimination will be eliminated. . . . The single market for 155,000,000 consumers will mean better quality coal and steel at lower prices. The coal and steel basin of Europe, hitherto divided among the nations, will be re-created into a single entity by gradual stages.

Wolf boy found

MEDICAL WORKERS IN LUCKNOW, India, were trying to help a nine-year-old 'wolf boy' found in January. He walked on all fours and behaved as if he had been reared by wild animals.

The new 1955 Ford 'Fairlane' sedan, as revealed to the world's press in November 1954. One of the main features of the latests Ford luxury cars was a wrap-around windscreen.

'Whatsoever a man soweth' by the cartoonist Vicky refers to South Africa's policy of Apartheid, which was five years old in 1954. Newly independent African states were reacting against the policy and there were discussions at the United Nations. South Africa withdrew from the UN General Assembly in 1955.

Whatsoever a man soweth

First NHS Health Centre

THE FIRST HEALTH CENTRE designed and built under the National Health Service was opened in Bristol on 16 September. (The UK Ministry of Health had reported earlier in the year on how improved health facilities were helping to lessen deaths among infants. Infant mortality per 1000 live births had fallen from 150 at the beginning of the century to 29.7 in 1951. By the 1980s, this had fallen much lower – to 11.)

Nkrumah triumphs

THE FIRST GENERAL ELECTIONS in the Gold Coast (now Ghana) conducted on a basis of direct voting throughout the country were held in June. Dr Kwame Nkrumah's Convention People's Party swept to victory. At a press conference, Nkrumah said his government would be 'Socialist in the same way as the British Labour Party' but there would be no nationalization.

A new Constitution in 1951 had given the Gold Coast greater responsibility over their own affairs than any other British colony in Africa. At the beginning of 1953, a Volta River Hydro-Electric and Aluminium Scheme was announced. The project aimed to develop the colony's water-power and bauxite resources with British support, to the advantage of both the UK and Gold Coast. The aluminium produced would guarantee the UK supplies at a competitive price.

Nehru's mixed economy

INDIA'S PRIME MINISTER NEHRU introduced in December a plan to nationalize the Imperial Bank of India and convert the country to a mixed economy. The idea was to nationalize basic industries and have private ownership of secondary industries. Widening public ownership was part of India's Five-Year Plan for Development 1951–6.

The government was also very concerned that large-scale industries should not hurt the efforts of small-scale village industries. A Community Development Programme was started in India in 1952, with 55 projects for the development of selected villages. The projects aimed to create more jobs and add to the skills of local people, while also improving health, agricultural production and education. As President Prasad said when the Programme started, the aim was to improve rural life since the population of India lived 'very largely in villages'. Prasad said:

At the project headquarters there will be experts in agriculture, engineering etc . . . for a group of villages there will be a village-level worker who will have a basic training in agricultural science and animal husbandry, supplemented by intensive training in extension methods and practices. He will be the carrier of the message to the door of the villager. . . . He will be intended to inspire people and to enlist their enthusiasm for a fuller life. . . .

India's Plan for 1951–6 also regarded land ownership as a key issue for national development. The Planning Commission that drafted the Plan thought there should be an absolute limit to the amount of land an individual could hold. A system of management was needed in which the land and other resources of villages could be developed for the widest benefits of communities. The Commission noted the importance of the village 'panchayat' in safeguarding the interests of landless peasants and in handling land reform. (The system of democratically elected village 'panchayats' or governments began in 1949. There had been forms of village government before this, but these were basically village elders assuming control and passing control to their sons.)

OAS Conference

THE TENTH CONFERENCE of the Organization of American States (OAS) met in Caracas, the capital of Venezuela, in March. Over 90 resolutions were adopted by the conference, the most important being a US call for joint inter-American action against Communism and an Argentinian resolution calling for the end of European colonies in the Western Hemisphere.

World statistics

THE UNITED NATIONS published statistics for the early 1950s, showing such facts as:
- UK newsprint production was 42% lower than it was before the Second World War.
- The USA and India were producing more feature films than any other country.
- The US had 52% of the world's radio sets, while 29% were in Europe and only about 1% were in Africa.
- Finland had the highest literacy rate in the world, with only about 1% of the population unable to read and write. By contrast, there were parts of Africa where only 1% of the population could read and write.

Lord of the Flies published

WILLIAM GOLDING'S novel about the cruel side of human nature was published in 1954. *Lord of the Flies* is the story of a group of boy evacuees. The aeroplane carrying them is wrecked on a desert island. The remains of the plane with pilot and other adults were all washed out to sea.

Ralph and the fat boy with glasses ('Piggy') find a conch shell. This is used to call the others for a meeting. Ralph is elected leader and he sends some boys to build shelters, others to make a fire. Jack and his group are the hunters of wild pigs to provide meat. Soon there is a breakdown of order and wild savagery results. Piggy is killed and Ralph nearly hunted to death before a ship arrives and rescues the boys.

'The tears began to flow and sobs shook him. He gave himself up to them now for the first time on the island; great, shuddering spasms of grief that seemed to wrench his whole body. . . . Ralph wept for the end of innocence, the darkness of man's heart, and the fall through the air of the true, wise friend called Piggy.'

Gymnastic triumph

AT THE WORLD CHAMPIONSHIPS the Japanese gymnastic team won two titles, with Keiko Ikeda performing outstandingly on the beam.

Bannister runs mile

ON 6 MAY a young English athlete and medical student competing in a race at Oxford became the first man to run the mile (1.6 km) in less than four minutes. Roger Bannister's time was 3 min. 59.4 seconds and he also set a new European record that year for the 500 metres.

Best plays and films

UNDER MILK WOOD by the Welsh poet Dylan Thomas was published. The play is about a day in the life of a small Welsh town.

The New York Drama Critics named *Teahouse of the August Moon* as the best American play of 1953–4.

A Star is Born, which premiered in October, tells the story of a failing marriage between two Hollywood stars. The career of one is just beginning while the other's is just ending. Judy Garland was the leading star.

On the Waterfront, starring Marlon Brando, opened in July. The film's mood is grim, describing corruption in the longshoreman's trade union.

In brief . . .

SWISS ARCHITECT LE CORBUSIER began designing a range of government buildings for India's new Punjabi capital of Chandigarh.

– Slinky film goddess Marilyn Monroe married former New York Yankees baseball star Joe Di Maggio.
– Henri Matisse, French painter, sculptor and designer of stained glass, died in Nice at the age of 94.
– Jorn Utzon's design for an Opera House to be built in Sydney, Australia was announced; it was an unusual design, conveying the feeling of white sails on the water.

Margot Fonteyn, leading ballerina, danced 'The Firebird' in London.

First polio vaccine

IN THE 1950s, poliomyelitis was still killing or paralysing thousands of children and young adults in richer Western countries. Then, in February 1954, a group of schoolchildren from Pittsburgh USA were innoculated with a serum against the disease. This was the first mass vaccination with the serum developed by Dr Jonas Salk. It contained polio virus that was killed with formalin. Widespread use of the Salk vaccine and Sabin vaccine (developed a few years later in 1957) have greatly reduced the threat of polio.

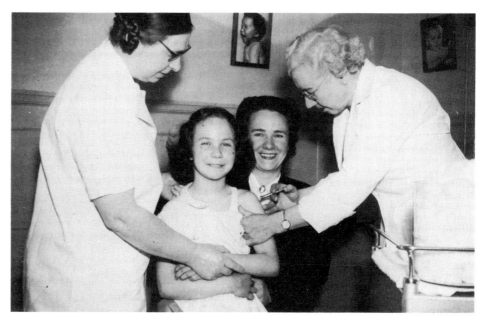

Polio vaccinations were first given in 1954 in America and 1956 in Britain. The photo shows one of the first children in the UK to benefit.

Nuclear reactor built

THE VERY FIRST NUCLEAR REACTOR to generate electricity was built in the USSR and started operation in June 1954. It used graphite as a moderator and produced a modest 5 megawatts of power – enough for a town of about 6000 people. The heat generated at the reactor's core was taken out by passing cooling water under high pressure through adjoining pipes. The water absorbed the heat of the core but did not boil because of its high pressure. The water then circulated through heat exchangers where it gave up its heat to a second, unpressurized water circuit. The water in this circuit boiled and produced steam, driving an electrical generator.

Smoking can cause cancer

IN JANUARY 1954 a tobacco industry committee was formed to investigate charges that cigarette smoking contributes to lung cancer. In June the American Cancer Society published the results of a 12-year study showing a significantly higher death rate amongst cigarette smokers than among non-smokers.

First transistor radio

AN AMERICAN COMPANY called Regency developed the first transistor radio in 1954 and was followed the next year by Sony in Japan. The earliest sets picked up only long and medium waves. Before the middle of the 1950s it was not possible to make a pocket-sized radio receiver. Valve sets were bulky and needed large batteries.

Mechanical translator

IN JANUARY, IBM demonstrated in New York a new 'mechanical translator', a machine for translating different languages.

First Eurovision programmes

AN IMPORTANT STEP in the international exchange of television programmes was taken in Western Europe in June and July 1954. Television programmes were successfully exchanged between 8 European countries. The European month began with a televised programme from Rome in which viewers in all the countries saw the Vatican and Pope Pius XII made a personal address.

(At the time, there was one television set for every 7 people in the USA, one for every 24 in the UK, one for every 55 people in Cuba, one for every 704 people in France and one for every 2400 in the Soviet Union.)

Civil Rights

Civil rights marchers in Washington DC.

Background to unrest

THE AMERICAN CIVIL WAR (1861–5) freed four million black slaves but there were soon laws segregating blacks from whites in the southern states. Black people were barred from white-only schools, hotels, restaurants, parks and other public facilities. In 1896 the Supreme Court had decided 'separate but equal' facilities were within the law. In fact these separate facilities were not equal. Housing and schools were of poorer quality and opportunities for work and job promotion were less.

Many southern blacks moved to northern cities but life was not much better for them there. In 1910 the National Association for the Advancement of Coloured People (NAACP) was formed. This Association worked towards more equal opportunities, but changes were very slow.

Bus boycotts

ROSA PARKS, a black seamstress, boarded a bus on 1 December 1955. The city was Montgomery, Alabama – one of many southern places where blacks were kept separate from whites. She paid her fare and sat in the first seat she found. She was 'bone weary' she recalled. As the bus filled up, other blacks went to the back of the bus as was the custom. The driver called out 'Niggers move back' but Mrs Parks didn't move. 'There was no plot', she

Laws such as poll taxes and literacy tests prevented most blacks from voting. In 1946 a President's Committee suggested reforms such as banning the poll tax and ending segregation. However Congress and much of the country was not yet ready to accept these ideas. Civil rights first became an important national issue in the 1950s.

explained later. 'I was just tired. My feet hurt.' The driver called a policeman and Mrs Parks was arrested.

News of her arrest angered the city's blacks. A group of twenty five black ministers met and led a one-day black boycott of the city buses. This led to more boycotts for black rights. Dr Martin Luther King Jr was the minister leading the campaigns. He became a major figure in the struggle for black equality, preaching non-violent protest to help change unjust laws. In 1956 the Supreme Court ruled that segregation on buses was unconstitutional. In 1957, Rev. King formed the Southern Christian Leadership Conference (SCLC) which led many campaigns for black rights. He warned white authorities 'we will wear you down by our capacity to suffer'. He trained his followers to put up with indignities, imprisonment, violence and even the threat of death.

Campaign

Integration of schools

CHANGE WAS ALSO TAKING PLACE in schools in the mid-1950s. In 1954, a black parent, Oliver Brown, took the Board of Education in Topeka, Kansas to the Supreme Court. His daughter was barred from attending the local white school. This was an important test case. On 17 May 1954, the Supreme Court ruled that segregation in schools was unconstitutional. Following this decision, four states (Delaware, Maryland, Missouri and West Virginia and the District of Colombia) started the process of integration. Four states (Georgia, Mississippi, Louisiana and South Carolina) remained strongly opposed. Arkansas, Alabama, Florida, Kentucky, Oklahoma, North Carolina, Tennessee, Texas and Virginia waited for further action by the Court before taking action themselves.

In April 1955, the Court held hearings to decide how its decision could be best implemented. A number of states argued it was impossible to change prejudice by a Court order and urged delay. On 31 May, the Court directed the States to make a 'prompt and reasonable' start towards implementing its ruling. Spokesmen in Georgia, South Carolina, Louisiana and Mississippi said they intended to continue with segregated schools. Governor Griffin of Georgia declared 'We shall continue to operate our schools as we have always operated them.'

A report published in December 1955 referred to 'hundreds of formerly segregated schools' which had been desegregated 'without creating serious tension or conflict.' The report also

More action in 1955

ANOTHER SUPREME COURT RULING came on 7 November 1955 saying that racial segregation in public parks, playgrounds, golf courses and bathing beaches was unconstitutional. The Court was dismissing the idea of 'separate but equal' facilities for blacks.

On 25 November, the Inter-State Commerce Commission ruled that racial segregation on inter-state trains and passenger buses and segregation of inter-state travellers in public waiting rooms were unlawful and must be ended by January 1956.

In December of 1955, delegates from twelve southern states met in secret in Memphis, Tennessee. Their plan was to start a new organization to fight racial integration. Court rulings helped move America towards greater equality, but it was not an easy move. (By 1963, only 9% of the South's school districts were integrated.)

It was the Court rulings and protests of the 1950s that led to the larger campaigns and rallies for civil rights in the 1960s.

noted that opponents of desegregation had resorted to 'economic pressure, intimidation and violence in some areas'.

The white parents of a civil rights worker who was murdered are comforted by blacks and other whites at a rally.

IAEA created

A NEW INTERNATIONAL ATOMIC ENERGY AGENCY was created in December 1955 by the UN General Assembly. This was part of President Eisenhower's 'atoms for peace' plan endorsed earlier in the year. The plan had also called for an international scientific conference on the peaceful uses of atomic energy.

The aims of the new IAEA were to (1) encourage world-wide research and development of the peaceful uses of atomic energy; (2) arrange for nuclear materials 'to meet the needs of research, development and practical application to all manner of peaceful activities, including the eventual production of power'; (3) foster the interchange of information on peaceful uses of atomic energy and (4) 'conduct its activities in such a way as to prepare for the time when the use of atomic energy for peace becomes the predominant and perhaps exclusive use of this great force.'

In December the UN General Assembly also established a 15-member scientific committee to study the effects of atomic radiation on man's health and environment.

Cumbernauld designated

A FIFTEENTH NEW TOWN, Cumbernauld, was designated by the Secretary of State for Scotland in July 1955. Under the New Towns Act of 1946 fourteen New Towns were designated to help relieve pressure of population on main British cities. By March 1955, over 33,000 dwellings had been built in the original 14 New Towns and another 11,000 homes were under construction. Cumbernauld was designated to relieve pressure on Glasgow and was intended to house 50,000 people.

Churchill resigns

ON 5 APRIL, SIR WINSTON CHURCHILL resigned as UK Prime Minister. Sir Anthony Eden became Prime Minister with Harold Macmillan as his Foreign Secretary.

On Churchill's departure, Clement Atlee spoke in the Commons:

Today we are parting with a Prime Minister who led this country through some of the most fateful years of Britain's history and who served in this House for more than 50 years. . . . He is going to have a well-earned rest. Instead of continuing to make history we hope he will continue to write it. . .

At the Conservative Conference in October, Eden said there could be no immediate cut in the two-year period of compulsory military service but the call-up age would be raised to 18 years five months in 1955 and to 19 years in 1956. He said of industrial relations:

I am anxious to see the growth of what I have often called partnership in industry. . . . I include in it joint consultation and the giving of full information to employees about the affairs of the companies in which they work. I also include profit-sharing . . . particularly when it offers opportunities for employees to hold shares and so acquire a real stake in the enterprise in which they work. . . . In this and other ways I believe that we can over the years bring greater peace throughout industry. . . .'

Winston Churchill is shown leaving 10 Downing Street and shaking hands with the new Prime Minister, Anthony Eden.

Coffee bureau established

COFFEE PRODUCERS in 15 South American countries met in New York and agreed to establish an International Coffee Bureau to help stabilize world coffee prices.

US crime increasing

FBI DIRECTOR J. EDGAR HOOVER reported an increase of over 26% in crime in the US since 1950, compared to a population rise of 7%.

Swedes drink freer

DRINK RATIONING IN SWEDEN had been in force since 1914 before it was abolished in 1955. The abolition of rationing allowed adults over age 21 to buy as much liquor as they wanted. Before 1955, the ration was 3 litres a month per person. Liquor also became freely available in restaurants.

Burgess, Maclean and Philby

AN ARTICLE IN A SUNDAY NEWSPAPER in 1955 alleged that Guy Burgess and Donald Maclean were long-term Soviet agents who had been recruited for spy work while still students at Cambridge, and that they had left Britain because they had learned that they were under investigation. A government White Paper was published in September 1955 in response. In December that year Foreign Secretary Harold Macmillan said in a Parliamentary debate on the Burgess-Maclean affair that no evidence had been found that Kim Philby was responsible for warning the two spies that their activities were arousing suspicion. Philby had strongly denied charges in 1952 but later defected to the Soviet Union where he lived as a confessed traitor to Britain until his death in 1988.
Sir Anthony Eden:

. . . Some have said that Burgess and Maclean should not have been prevented from escaping unless a charge could have been preferred. . . British justice over the centuries has been based on the principle that a man is innocent until he can be proved guilty. Have we got to abandon that principle? . . .

Hair styles such as the 'bebop' and 'back sweep' were fashionable for young men. The popular D.A. worn by these boys was named for resembling the back-side of a duck.

Lolita published

NOVELIST VLADIMIR NABOKOV was born in Russia in 1899 but left after the Revolution to live in Western Europe and then went to America in 1940. *Lolita* is the story of a European refugee in America who is obsessively attracted to a young girl of twelve. To be near Lolita, the central character marries her mother who is then killed in an accident. He and Lolita travel, and when she is seduced by an old playwright, he murders the playwright.

The book excells in describing the neon-lit American scene and some readers accused it of being anti-American. ('. . . There is nothing louder than an American hotel; and, mind you, this was supposed to be a quiet, cosy, old-fashioned, homey place – "gracious living" and all that stuff.') Nabokov defended his book, saying it was not immoral nor against the USA. 'I chose American motels instead of Swiss hotels or English inns only because I am trying to be an American writer. . . . It is childish to study a work of fiction in order to gain information about a country or about a social class. . . .'

Rebel Without a Cause

THE FILM *Rebel Without a Cause* premiered in New York, starring James Dean. Later that year he died in a car crash, having been in Hollywood only a year and having acted in only three films. Dean became a symbol of youth rebellion and he continued to be idolized long after his death.

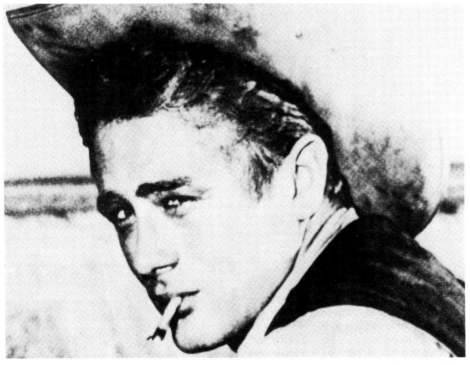

Cinema star James Dean died in a car accident after only three films but became a hero of the new youth culture.

New Disney films

DAVY CROCKETT, KING OF THE WILD FRONTIER was a new Walt Disney film in 1955, sparking a craze for racoon skin-style hats with tails, as worn by woodsmen in America's pioneer days. *Lady and the Tramp* appeared as a new feature-length cartoon.

Poetry award

EDWARD ESTLIN (E.E.) Cummings won the 1955 National Book Award for his *Poems* 1923–54. His verse was known for its eccentric use of typography and punctuation. He made wide use of slang, dialect and the rhythms of jazz in his work.

'Pop Art' coined

THE TERM 'POP ART' was coined in the mid-1950s by an English critic. The style blossomed in the late 1950s in New York and later spread around the US and Europe.

One of the first Pop artists was Robert Rauschenberg, an American painter who gained recognition in 1953. His complex collages were known as 'combine paint'. He used real objects on the canvas, with a mixture of painting techniques. Materials such as torn posters and children's drawings might also be incorporated.

Motor racing disaster

TRAGEDY STRUCK LE MANS in 1955 when a serious accident left many spectators dead. The accident had many repercussions – including a permanent ban on motor racing in Switzerland.

The American atomic submarine Nautilus, *which made an historic voyage under the North Pole.*

First nuclear-powered submarine

THE *NAUTILUS*, the world's first nuclear-powered submarine, was built in 1955 for the US Navy. In its first two years, the submarine travelled 62,000 miles without refuelling. In 1958, the Nautilus made an epic voyage from Point Barrow Alaska to the Greenland Sea, crossing the North Pole on 3 August.

Scientists warn of nuclear threat

IN JULY 1955, a group of world famous people appealed for warfare to end. They also warned about the dangers of thermonuclear explosions. Amongst the group were eminent scientists such as Albert Einstein and Bertrand Russell.

Fibre optics applied

THE VERY FIRST APPLICATION of fibre optics was in Britain in 1955. Dr Narinder S. Kapany designed a new type of light guide made from tiny strands of glass called optical fibre.

Each strand of the light guide was the diameter of a human hair and made from two types of glass. When light was shone down one end, it bounced its way down the full length of the strand.

Optical fibres are now used in such fields as medicine, with devices like the endoscope allowing doctors to see right into the body. The fibres are also used in telecommunications.

IGY announced

DETAILED PLANS were revealed in early 1955 for a world-wide co-ordinated study of natural phenomena. Forty nations were to co-operate in International Geophysical Year, to last 18 months from 1 July 1957 to 31 December 1958. Each country planned its own programme under a wider plan by a central co-ordinating committee.

Studies were made in such areas as meteorology and climate, cosmic rays and glaciology. The world was divided into six regions for the purpose of investigation. Over 20 observation stations were established by 11 countries on the Antarctic continent, where studies were carried out on a wide scale. Research into the upper atmosphere was carried out by thousands of instrument-carrying balloons and scores of rockets.

The British Astronomer-Royal, Sir Harold Spencer Jones, described it as:

the largest scheme for international co-operation in science that has ever been planned. . . . Special methods of observation will be used to supplement observation from the ground. Balloons . . . will be widely used and will carry recording equipment that will telemeter information back to the ground. . . . Important additional data will be obtained by the use of rockets, which can carry 150 lb of equipment to heights of 125 miles . . . three regions of the globe are of special importance in geophysical investigation: the Arctic, the Antarctic and the Equatorial belt.

US mental health

THE HOOVER COMMISSION studying US Medical Services said in March that mental illness was the greatest single US health problem, with 6% of the population suffering from some form of mental disorder.

Sun heat

IN 1955, the first solar-powered hot-water system was built, in Israel.

Canal nationalized

THE SUEZ CANAL was built over ten years under the direction of a French engineer. It opened on 17 November 1869 and was run by the Suez Canal Company, based in Paris. The Canal is 103 miles (166km) long, running along the desert from Port Said to Suez. In 1873 the British Prime Minister Disraeli bought 176,602 of the Canal shares for Britain. The Company has had a majority of foreign shareholders and under the Convention of 1888 all nations were guaranteed free use on the Canal.

In the mid-1950s, a crisis developed over ownership and use of this vital waterway. In 1952, King Farouk (1920-65) of Egypt was forced to abdicate by an army revolt. The President of the new republic was Gamal Abdel Nasser (1918-70), who took office in 1954. Nasser made an arms deal with Czechoslovakia in 1955 and also received an Anglo-US offer of financial help for building the Aswan Dam. In July 1956, Britain and the US withdrew their Aswan Dam offer. They had become concerned about Egypt's pro-Communist sympathies. Nasser's reply was to nationalize the private Suez Canal Company.

On 26 July, Nasser made a speech saying that income from the Canal would be used to build the Dam:

We shall build the High Dam on the skulls of . . . Egyptian workmen who died in building the Suez Canal . . . Egypt will build the Aswan Dam without pressure from any nation.

In his bitter attack on the Western nations, Nasser said there had been a 'conspiracy' to 'trick' Egypt into building the Dam and then to 'impose conditions on Egypt affecting her independence and integrity.' A statement on 31 July gave assurances that freedom of navigation on the Canal would not be affected by the nationalization. As Nasser said: 'no one would be more interested than Egypt in the freedom of passage through the Canal. We are certain that traffic through the Canal will in the coming years justify all our hopes and those of the whole world. . .'

British protest

THE BRITISH PROTESTED strongly on 27 July, saying that '. . . H.M. Government protests against this arbitrary action which constitutes a serious threat to the freedom of navigation on a waterway of vital international importance. . .'. Cairo Radio announced the same evening that the Egyptian government had refused to accept the British Note. The Note had been sent after a day of much political activity in London. Sir Anthony Eden's statement to the House of Commons said: 'This unilateral decision of the Egyptian Government to expropriate the Suez Canal Company without notice and in breach of the concessions agreements affects the rights and interests of many nations. . .'

On 28 July, the British Treasury took financial measures against Egypt. A directive forbade the transfer of any cash, securities or gold belonging to the Suez Canal Company in the UK without the Treasury's consent. The second measure forbade transfers into or out of Egyptian sterling accounts in the UK without Treasury permission.

The British Embassy in Cairo advised British nationals living in Egypt to consider leaving and the French Embassy gave similar advice to French nationals. France too had strongly denounced Egypt's action over the canal. America also took actions against Egypt.

National newspapers in Britain for 31 October, 1956.

Suez

In November, ships at the entrance to the Canal at Port Said were sunk by the Egyptians.

European action

ON 29 JULY, the US, France and Britain began Three-Power discussions on the Suez Crisis. The talks ended on 2 August when a communiqué was issued. The Statement included the following:

. . . the present action involves far more than a simple act of nationalization. It involves the arbitrary and unilateral seizure by one nation of an international agency which has the responsibility to maintain and operate the Suez Canal so that all the signatories to, and beneficiaries of, the Treaty of 1888 can effectively enjoy the use of an international waterway upon which the economy, commerce and security of much of the world depends. . .

Acknowledged threat

AN INTERNATIONAL CONFERENCE was proposed to consider the establishment of an international agency to govern the Suez Canal and assure free use for all countries. The London Conference on the Suez Canal opened on 16 August, with only two invited countries – Egypt and Greece – refusing to attend. The British Foreign Secretary, Selwyn Lloyd, had broadcast a speech on 14 August saying the Suez situation was the third and most serious international crisis since the Second World War:

I do not want to sound alarmist but a threat to the Suez Canal is a threat to the life and strength of Britain and of Western Europe on one side and to the countries of Asia on the other. . . . The Suez Canal Company is not just an Egyptian company. . . . It was formed for an international purpose. It is internationally owned. Its administration is

centred outside Egypt. A company possessing such an international character cannot lawfully be nationalized in the way in which that has been done. . .

Meanwhile, other Arab countries and those in Eastern Europe were supporting Egypt. President Tito of Yugoslavia maintained that Egypt had the full sovereign right to nationalize the Canal.

In October, hostilities began between Egypt and Israel. Britain and France were even more anxious about the Canal and sent in forces to the Canal zone. The United Nations called for a cease-fire and put its forces on the Egypt-Israeli border. Also in October a new Suez Canal Users' Association (SCUA) was formed. The dispute and various suggestions for settlement continued. By 1957, the Suez Canal was re-opened to all shipping.

Hungarian revolution

IN THE 1950S, the countries of Eastern Europe under Communist control began asserting themselves against USSR power. East Berliners rioted in June 1953 and there were riots in Poznan, Poland in 1956. The Polish Communist leader, Wladyslaw Gomulka, was able to secure more independence.

A revolution broke out in Hungary in October 1956. Students and workers were fighting against Soviet control. The Hungarian Communist Party asked for Soviet help in dealing with the rebellion and bitter battles took place with troops sent in by Russia. Large areas of Budapest, the capital, were devastated. Tens of thousands of Hungarians were killed or wounded and Russian soldiers were casualties as well. There was near-famine and conditions were chaotic.

A special correspondent for the *Daily Telegraph* reported:

I drove slowly through the centre of the city soon after dawn today. It was like a front-line strongpoint in a major military compaign. Tanks blockaded the main Danube bridges and covered all principal cross-roads. Burnt-out lorries and cars lay on their sides in the streets. Broken glass glistened on the pavement and the smashed cable wires of the tram system trailed on the ground. . . . From what I have seen and been told there is no doubt that the spearhead of the revolt was in units of the Hungarian Regular Army itself. . . . The most impossible thing to convey out of the tragic Budapest scene, yet the most important, is the choking hate of the ordinary people against their present masters and the Russians who protect them. . .

On 24 October the Central Committee of the Hungarian Workers' Party confirmed the appointment of Imre Nagy as Prime Minister. He announced sweeping reforms with Soviet troops to be withdrawn from Budapest, political prisoners to be

released and the one-party system abolished. Hungary withdrew from the Warsaw pact and appealed to the UN for help. This was all too much for the USSR who sent tanks and troops into Budapest on 4 November to suppress the revolution. A pro-Soviet government was put into office. Nagy was later captured and put to death.

Many nations held demonstrations and protested at Soviet actions. Some leading British Communists even resigned from the party. Peter Fryer resigned from the Communist *Daily Worker* newspaper after it refused to publish his reports from Hungary. He said at the time:

No honest Communist can ignore the truth about Hungary. The Hungarian people were the victims of tyranny and oppression masquerading as Socialism. . . The whole police dictatorship was so rotten and so universally detested that it collapsed like a house of cards the instant the people rose to their feet. . . But their hopes were crushed by Soviet intervention.

Speaking at the UN in late November, Lester Pearson of Canada said that the UN had 'witnessed in Hungary one of the greatest betrayals in history.' By its armed intervention and its 'shameless disregard of its obligations under the Charter', the Soviet Union had not only killed Hungarians but had betrayed the principles and ideals of the UN.

There was a mass exodus of refugees from Hungary, over 100,000 by 1 December. Despite Soviet control of the frontier, many managed to cross into Austria at great risk to their lives. The US, Britain and other countries took in these refugees.

Hungarians drove through the streets of the capital Budapest at the height of anti-Communist demonstrations.

Russian leader Nikita Khrushchev shown here on his visit to London in 1956.

Khrushchev denounces Stalin

NIKITA KHRUSHCHEV gave an important speech to the 20th Congress of the Soviet Communist Party in February 1956. His 26,000 words denouncing Stalin were published some months later in US and British newspapers. Khrushchev described the brutal purges and harshness of the man:

'. . . Stalin was a very distrustful man; . . . He could look at a man and say "Why are your eyes so shifty today?" or "Why are you avoiding looking me directly in the eyes?" This sickly suspicion created in him a general distrust even towards eminent party workers whom he had known for years. Everywhere and in everything he saw "enemies","two-facers" and "spies". . .

'Stalin very energetically popularized himself as a great leader. In various ways he tried to inculcate in the people the version that all victories gained by the Soviet nation during the war were due to the courage, daring and genius of Stalin, and of no-one else. . .

'You see to what Stalin's mania for greatness led. He had completely lost consciousness of reality; he demonstrated his suspicion and haughtiness not only in relation to individuals in the USSR but in relation to whole nations. . .

We must abolish the cult of the individual decisively. . .'

In brief . . .

<u>January:</u> A new railway opened through Outer Mongolia linking China and Russia. Sudan was proclaimed an independent democratic republic.

<u>March:</u> Tunisia and Morocco became independent countries.

<u>May:</u> Celebrations throughout India marked the 2,500th anniversary of Buddhism.

<u>July:</u> The International Finance Corporation (IFC) was formed by the World Bank.

US President Eisenhower and leaders of 18 Latin American countries met in Panama and signed a declaration of common principles.

<u>October:</u> Representatives of 82 nations met in Geneva to establish an international agency to promote the peaceful use of atomic energy.

Beat generation

IN THE MID-1950S, 'beatniks' appeared in America rebelling against the restrictions of society. The Beats, as they were known, were poets and artists on the east and west coasts. Their work protested against the commercialism and uniformity of American life. Allen Ginsberg's poem 'Howl' was published in 1956 and was typical of the style:

I saw the best minds of my generation destroyed by madness,
starving hysterical naked,
dragging themselves through the negro streets at dawn
looking for an angry fix . . .

Jack Kerouac's novel *On the Road* published in 1957 also reflected the bohemian spirit of the time.

Beckett's *Godot*

IRISH novelist and playwright Samuel Beckett first produced *Waiting for Godot* in French in 1952. The English version was a theatrical highlight of 1956. Beckett's world is stark and seemingly pointless, with characters unable to communicate. The play is both amusing and tragic with lines like 'We are all born mad. Some remain so.'

In *Waiting for Godot*, there are tramps arguing amidst heavy Christian symbolism. The tree under which the tramps wait and on which they think of hanging themselves could be several trees. Is it the Tree of Knowledge, the Tree of Life, or the wood on which Jesus died? 'We're waiting for Godot – You're sure it was here? – What? – That we were to wait? – He said by the tree . . .' The play is both of hope and despair. Is it worth waiting if Godot doesn't come? Another famous Beckett play *Endgame* appeared in 1957.

Osborne play performed

LOOK BACK IN ANGER by English playwright John Osborne was first performed in 1956. It was the first outstandingly successful play at the Royal Court Theatre in London. The story is of a young working-class man who protests against middle-class attitudes in society. The play started a new kind of realistic drama, with Osborne and others becoming known as 'angry young men'.

Playwright John Osborne, part of the Fifties movement of 'angry young men'.

Marciano retires

HEAVYWEIGHT BOXER Rocky Marciano retired in 1956, unbeaten after 49 professional bouts. Five world heavyweight champions have retired while still holding the title, but only Marciano retired undefeated.

Premieres

Film version of Rogers and Hammerstein's musical *Carousel*
Film version of *The King and I*
Film version of *Around the World in 80 Days*

Published

Jazz singer Billie Holiday's autobiography *Lady Sings the Blues*.
Meyer Levin's novel *Compulsion*, based on the famous Leopold-Loeb murder trial.

Monroe marries Miller

FILM STAR MARILYN MONROE married playwright Arthur Miller in June. She was in her height of glamorous fame in the mid-1950s. The Motion Picture Almanac published a poll determining the top US money-making stars of the year. Monroe was the female winner in 1953, 1954, 1956 and 1957.

Cricket record

ENGLAND BOWLER Jim Laker took 46 wickets in the Test Series against Australia in 1956. This record performance was the best ever and earned him a great reputation.

Amniocentesis

AN UNBORN BABY in a womb is surrounded by fluid. This liquid can be tested by pushing a needle in through the abdomen and withdrawing a sample. Fluid samples can be tested chemically to discover such diseases as spina bifida in the foetus. Fluid cells can be viewed microscopically to see if abnormalities like Down's Syndrome are present. This 'amniocentesis' (testing of the amniotic fluid) was first routinely performed in Manchester in 1956 to detect jaundice. Such early testing allows a woman with a very abnormal foetus the chance to choose abortion. It may be possible in the future to give some treatments to foetuses before birth.

Seeding clouds

US PRESIDENT EISENHOWER'S Commission on Weather Control reported in March increases of 9-17 per cent in precipitation from clouds seeded with dry ice or silver iodide in recent tests.

Gas-cooled reactor

THE VERY FIRST large-scale nuclear power plant was opened at Calder Hall in Cumbria in 1956. The reactor was moderated by graphite and cooled by carbon dioxide gas under pressure, instead of water. The fuel was natural (unenriched) uranium held inside long tubes ('cans') made of Magnox, an alloy of magnesium. These cans were held in place by a grid so that gas could be blown in between to withdraw heat produced by fission. Hot gas moved through water boilers, producing steam which generated electricity.

Britain chose gas cooling for several reasons. One was the fear of dangers caused by water-cooled reactors. If the water in the reactor acid boils and turns to steam, the fuel elements will be left uncooled. They will overheat and melt, wrecking the reactor and possibly allowing harmful radiation to escape. This cannot happen with gas because it does not change its physical state, whatever the temperature. France also initially chose gas-cooled graphite-moderated reactors.

Calder Hall in Cumbria was the world's first full-scale atomic power station.

Synthetic diamonds

THE FIRST DIAMONDS ever to be produced by laboratory process were shown to scientists on 15 February 1956 at the General Electric Research Station in New York.

Synthetic diamonds were produced by simulating pressures and temperatures at a depth of 240 miles (384 km) below the surface of the earth. A special vessel contained within a 1000-ton hydraulic press had maintained for relatively long periods pressures greater than 100,000 atmospheres (i.e. 1,500,000 pounds force per square inch) or 100,000 kg force per square centimetre and temperatures above 5000 degrees Fahrenheit (2777 degrees Celsius).

The basic constituent of the synthetic diamonds was carbon, as in the case of natural diamonds. However, man-made diamonds were very small compared with natural diamonds and the Director of Research pointed out it would be 'decidedly premature' to conclude 'that we are about to make diamonds of a size and quality suitable for gem use'.

Videotape recorder

THE FIRST practical videotape recorder for television pictures was made by Ampex Corporation in California in 1956. This was originally for broadcasters wanting to save pictures for transmitting later but has led to the development of home video cassette recorders.

Picture phones

BELL TELEPHONE Laboratories announced in August the development of a 'picture phone' that transmits pictures as well as voices of people talking by phone.

Sputnik

First space satellite

'SPACE AGE IS HERE' shouted the *Daily Express* headlines on 5 October 1957.

Man entered the Space Age yesterday when Russia rocketed an earth satellite – a man-made 'moon' – into outer space. It is now circling the world 560 miles up once every 95 minutes. Tass, the Soviet news agency, reported that the satellite could be viewed in the rays of the rising and setting sun using ordinary binoculars.

This launch of Sputnik I, the first artificial satellite, astounded the world. Sputnik established that space travel was possible. It also showed that Russia could make an intercontinental missile capable of reaching America. The space race was on and Russia clearly was in the lead.

Sputnik I was filled with steel radio transmitters which emitted signals. People around the world noticed a mysterious bleep from their radio and television sets, which created some fear until Russia announced what it had done. A mere 22.8 inches (58cm) in diameter and weighing just 184 pounds (83.5kg), Sputnik I was equipped to record and transmit data about the atmosphere.

On 6 October the *Observer* commented:

. . . Western scientists were still feeling rather dazed yesterday at the Russian achievement. The most extraordinary feature is the satellite's reported weight . . . since every extra pound of satellite adds 1000 lb to the weight of the rocket needed to fire it into orbit, the Russians must have used a truly colossal launching rocket. . . . It must have weighed at least 80 tons whereas the US satellite launching rocket will weigh about 10 tons. But the American engineers have been having trouble in getting even a launcher of this size to work reliably . . .

American attempt

IN DECEMBER, the United States tried to put a Vanguard satellite into orbit, weighing just three pounds (1.4 kg). In contrast to Russian secrecy, America's launch at Cape Canaveral, Florida was much publicized. The rocket 'toppled slowly, breaking apart . . . with a tremendous roar'. Senator Lyndon B. Johnson described the failure as 'one of the best publicized and most humiliating in our history. . . I shrink a little inside of me whenever the US announces a great event – and it blows up in our face.'

This embarrassing failure caused America to question for the first time whether its science and education really was the best in the world. In 1958, Congress passed a National Defense Education Act, NDEA, which authorized $1 billion for federal and state education programmes providing new equipment for schools, loans for college students, fellowships and special programmes in the sciences, mathematics and foreign languages. Another effect of Sputnik was to greatly increase the influence of America's scientists in government and policy making. The office of Special Assistant to the President for Science and Technology was established in 1958.

Sputnik II

WITHIN A MONTH of Sputnik I, Russia rocketed Sputnik II into space. This carried a black and white husky dog Laika as a passenger. The Soviet News Agency Tass broadcast:

By the successful launching of the second artificial earth satellite, with diverse scientific instruments and an experimental animal, Soviet scientists are extending the programme of studying cosmic space and the upper layers of the atmosphere. The unfathomed natural processes going on in the cosmos will now become more understandable to man.

The second satellite weighed half a ton – six times as much as the first Sputnik. Until 5 November, when the satellite had completed over a million miles (1,609 million km), Moscow Radio bulletins had announced that the dog's condition was still satisfactory and its pulse and respiration normal. After that date, however, no further mention was made of Laika by Moscow radio and it was thought that the dog might be no longer alive. Animal lovers in many countries made strong protests. A group from the Canine Defence League called at the Soviet Embassy in London saying there could be 'no justification for submitting this dog to such an ordeal. . . . The horror induced in the mind of the dog can never be known, just as no explanation of the purpose of the journey can be made to her.' The League Against Cruel Sports expressed its 'horror, disgust and contempt' at the Russian experiment. Sputnik II circled the earth for six months.

Launched

Race for space begun

SPUTNIK proved that the Soviet Union could produce rockets and long-range armed missiles more powerful than those America had. The American ballistic missile programme was speeded up. The arms race and the space race became part of the same race for the best technology. America did launch its first artificial satellite in 1958 (see p. 59).

Early satellites could stay up only a short time – Sputnik I was in orbit for only 62 days. When a satellite orbits the earth, air resistance causes it to lose energy so that it spirals downwards towards the ground. Modern satellites are fitted with tiny rockets to keep them from wandering off station, carrying enough fuel to operate their rockets for up to seven years.

The missile carrying the Sputnik I satellite soars into space. Since 1957, satellites have provided many benefits, including adding to our knowledge of the earth's shape, mapping the magnetic field surrounding earth, photographing the far side of the moon, making possible global TV and telephone transmission, weather monitoring and tracing nuclear explosions.

Giant Soviet rockets using five separate liquid-fuel engines were developed in the mid-1950s. Only in the 1960s did USA develop launch vehicles that were as powerful.

49

World News

EEC is formed

THE FIRST ATTEMPTS at an economic union for Western Europe began in the 1950s. A European Coal and Steel Community was formed in 1952 by France, West Germany, Italy, Belgium, the Netherlands and Luxemborg. The idea was expanded in 1957 and the same countries established the European Economic Community (EEC). Customs duties between the member states were lowered and a common market was set up with a single tariff on imports. The European Parliament was formed the following year (1958).

Italian representatives signed the Treaty of Rome on 25 March, marking the birth of the EEC.

Little Rock, Arkansas, USA. White students at Central High School walked past armed guardsmen whose job was to keep black students from registering at the school.

Malaya independent

THE INDEPENDENT Federation of Malaya became official on 31 August (Merdeka Day). Malayan, British and Commonwealth troops took part in ceremonies where the Union Jack was formally taken down after 83 years of British rule. The Malayan flag was hoisted to the music of 'Negara Ku' ('My Country'). The Duke of Gloucester read a message from the Queen welcoming Malaya 'with deep and real pleasure to the brotherhood of our Commonwealth family of nations'.

Little Rock struggle

SOME OF America's states continued to resist racial integration. One famous example was the school board of Little Rock, Arkansas, who were ordered to integrate in 1957. Crowds of white parents and pupils tried to stop black children going into white schools. One sixteen year-old black girl described her experience:

The crowd moved in closer and began to follow me, calling me names . . . somebody started yelling 'lynch her'. . . . They came closer, shouting 'no nigger bitch is going to get in our school! Get out of here!'

The Arkansas State Governor, Orval Faubus, also resisted integration. He and most southern whites believed in 'States Rights' – each state deciding for itself. Faubus broke the law by bringing in the National Guard to stop the black children entering Little Rock High School. President Eisenhower sent troops to the school to restore order and black children were finally able to enter.

Also in 1957, Congress passed a civil rights law that allowed the Federal Government to move against some forms of discrimination in the registration of voters.

First BBC TV schools broadcast

AN ILLUSTRATED TALK on British Columbia was the very first BBC television broadcast to schools, on 24 September 1957. There were five broadcasts each week on 'Living in the Empire' as well as broadcasts on science, current affairs and 'Young People at Work'.

Channel tunnel revived

THE IDEA of having a tunnel beneath the English Channel linking Britain to the European continent had been discussed for years. It was revived in 1957 and at a general meeting of the Channel Tunnel Co. Ltd Mr d'Erlanger said:

It would seem that this old and hoary subject is at last emerging into something which has now to be considered seriously. . . . We in Britain so far from considering a Channel Tunnel to be a threat to our island today are coming round to the view that our economic and military security will in the future depend upon closer integration with the Continent.

World population

IN MAY 1957 a UN Demographic Yearbook estimated the world's population at 2,691,000,000 – about half the total number at the end of the 1980s.

Clean air act

A NEW Clean Air Act in the UK in 1957 gave local authorities the power to create smoke control areas in which it would be an offence to emit smoke from buildings. The Act further authorized them to make by-laws requiring new buildings to have 'smokeless' heating and cooking arrangements. Owners or occupiers of existing houses in 'smoke control areas' could receive grants of at least 70 per cent of the cost of adapting or replacing grates or stoves for smokeless fuel.

'Eisenhower Doctrine'

PRESIDENT EISENHOWER put forward a new Middle Eastern policy in January, saying that the US would permit no Communist conquests in the Middle East:

Russia's rulers have long sought to dominate the Middle East. The reason for Russia's interest in the Middle East is solely that of power politics . . . the policy which I outline involves certain burdens and, indeed, risks for the United States. Those who covet the area will not like what is proposed.

President Eisenhower's proposals for American military and economic aid to Middle Eastern countries threatened by Communism were approved by the Senate in March. Secretary of State Dulles said:

You may feel that there . . . is no doubt as to what Congress would do if international Communism set out on piecemeal conquest of the world by war. But until Congress has actually spoken, there is doubt in the Middle East and there may be doubt in the Soviet Union. . .

Home guard disbanded again

BRITAIN'S HOME GUARD was again disbanded in 1957. It was originally formed as the Local Defence Volunteers in May 1940 when it seemed that Germans would invade. The name was changed to the Home Guard in July 1940. The force, which consisted of men too old or too young for active service, played a useful part in Britain's defence. The Guard was first disbanded after the Second World War then reformed in 1952 at the time of the Korean war.

The Birthday Party appears

HAROLD PINTER'S first full-length play was produced in 1957. The play is set in a shabby boarding house at the edge of an ocean, where the only boarder is Stanley until two new male guests arrive. They say they have come to do a 'job'. The tension mounts as the two men question Stanley. The owner of the house, Meg, suggests a birthday party for Stanley and he is later taken away by the men. This early Pinter play is typical in having a sense of anxiety in an enclosed place, usually one room. Critics at the time were puzzled by the many illogical conversations in the play.

French writer Albert Camus (1913-60) explaining his existentialist ideas.

Camus wins Nobel Prize

PHILOSOPHICAL French writer Albert Camus won the 1957 Nobel Prize for Literature with *The Fall* ('La Chute'). Camus believed that the universe is irrational, or what existentialists call 'absurd'. His earlier novels included *The Stranger* ('L'Etranger'), and *The Plague* ('La Peste'). In *The Fall* Camus explores moral responsibility. ('I shall tell you a great secret, my friend. Do not wait for the last judgement. It takes place every day.') The 'Fall' is man's spiritual fall, and Camus's book was very popular with Catholics. Camus's novel also explores more mundane aspects of life: 'You know what charm is: a way of getting the answer yes without having asked any clear question.'

Triumphant fifth

ARGENTINIAN racing driver Juan Fangio won his fifth world title and then went into semi-retirement aged 46.

Sack dress

FASHION turned loose in 1957, with full unwaisted dresses. These 'sack' or 'trapeze' styles followed on from the 'letter shapes' of the mid-1950s. (In 1954-55, the designer Dior produced H-line, A-line and Y-line dresses and the ideas were copied into high-street fashion.)

1957 was also the first year of the stiletto heel and shoes with narrowly pointed toes.

High jump shoe

A CONTROVERSIAL built-up shoe was introduced to European high jumping in 1957. The 2 inch (5 cm) thick sole enabled new world records to be set but the shoe was banned in 1958 by the International Amateur Athletic Federation. The principle of the shoe was similar to the prop used by Watusi tribesmen of Central Africa. They reportedly cleared heights of 8 feet 2½ inches (250 cm) in ceremonial jumps by leaping from a small mound of earth.

West Side Story

LEONARD BERNSTEIN'S musical *West Side Story* opened in New York, transferring the story of Romeo and Juliet to the slums of the city. Teenage gangs called the 'Sharks' and 'Jets' acted out the rivalry between native Americans and Puerto Rican immigrants.

Pressurized water reactor (PWR)

AN AMERICAN-DESIGNED nuclear reactor used enriched uranium fuel elements immersed in water under high pressure. The water acts both as a moderator and as a coolant. The pressurized water does not boil but passes through a heat exchanger to raise steam. This system is known as a pressurized water reactor (PWR).

The first PWR to be used for generating electricity was built at Shippingport, Pennsylvania in 1957. Since then, PWR has been the most successful design of reactor, selling in many parts of the world. PWR is simple and extracts a lot of power from a relatively small reactor. It is therefore relatively cheap to build but there are disadvantages. The PWR needs safety equipment to supply emergency cooling if the normal cooling circuits fail. These emergency core-cooling systems have been the subject of much controversy.

Windscale overheats

THE NUCLEAR REACTOR at Britain's Windscale plutonium producing plant in Cumbria overheated in October. Radioactive iodine escaped, contaminating an area of 200 square miles (518 square kilometers) around the plant. The two Windscale reactors were shut down and all local milk supplies were destroyed following the incident.

In brief . . .

FIRST ELECTRIC WRISTWATCH marketed (USA)
First portable electric typewriter (USA)

Diagram of a Pressurized Water Reactor.

Atomic news

IN JANUARY 1957, the Chairman of the National Academy of Science's Committee on Genetic Effects of Atomic Radiation warned that 6000 handicapped children would be born in the current generation due to radioactive effects of nuclear weapons tests.

The British Atomic Scientists Association published a report in April warning that weapons tests may 'even produce bone cancer in 1000 people for every million tons of TNT' yielded by the tests. California Institute of Technology chemist Linus Pauling said that 10,000 people were dying or had died of leukemia throughout the world as a result of nuclear weapons tests. He warned that planned British tests would result in another 1000 leukemia cases.

In September the Atomic Energy Commission detonated the first recorded underground nuclear explosion in a chamber beneath a 7000 foot mountain at the Nevada proving grounds.

Borazon discovered

A NEW man-made material called Borazon was discovered in 1957, at the same New York State Research Laboratory where synthetic diamonds were accomplished in 1956 (see p.47). Borazon is harder than diamonds and is able to stand more than twice as much heat. Scientists pointed out that Borazon was the hardest substance ever made by man and might replace diamonds in some industrial uses. While a diamond burned at about 1600 degrees F., (871 degrees C.) Borazon did not melt until temperatures of over 4000 degrees F. (2204 degrees C.) were reached.

PRESSURIZED WATER REACTOR

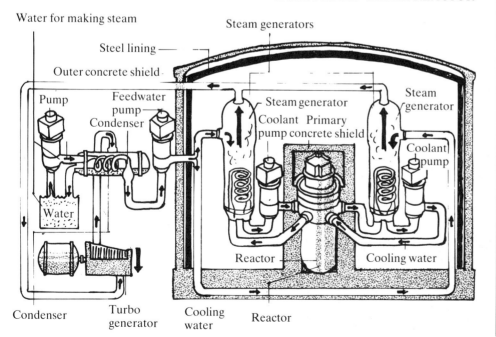

Water for making steam
Steam generators
Steel lining
Outer concrete shield
Pump
Feedwater pump
Condenser
Steam generator
Coolant Primary pump concrete shield
Steam generator
Coolant pump
Water
Reactor
Cooling water
Condenser
Turbo generator
Cooling water
Reactor

1958   King Elvis

Elvis 'The King'

ELVIS PRESLEY, 'the King of Rock 'n' Roll' became a private in the US Army in 1958. In a few short years he had become a symbol of youth rebellion as well as adored by millions of fans. The son of a poor Southern farmworker, Elvis rose from his humble childhood to be a multi-millionaire.

His mother had always told him that he was just as good as anyone else. When she died in 1958, Elvis stood with his father on the steps of Graceland, the mansion he had bought in 1957. 'Look Daddy', Elvis sobbed, pointing to the chicken his mother had kept on the lawn of the hundred thousand-dollar mansion, 'Mama won't never feed them chickens no more.'

Rise to fame

IT WAS as a present for his mother that Elvis paid four dollars in the early 1950s to record an acetate disc with two songs. The owner of the Sun Recording Co. liked Elvis's singing and gave him a chance to make a record for general release in 1954 ('That's All Right Mama'). Then in 1956 Presley became first a national and then an international sensation. He appeared on the Tommy and Jimmy Dorsey television show early that year singing 'Blue Suede Shoes' and 'Heartbreak Hotel'. Soon 'Heartbreak Hotel' was number one in the US music charts and Presley mania had begun.

Elvis Presley, known as the King of rock 'n' roll.

Adults were shocked by Elvis's mean, sexy image and his gyrations. Many said he was a bad influence and tried to ban his appearances. The younger generation, newly called 'teenagers', liked him all the more for shocking their parents. His style was that of a lower class 'hoodlum' or 'hood'. Presley's hair was slicked back into a 'duck-ass' or 'd-a' shape, with long sideburns. Greasy levis, motorcycle boots, t-shirts and black leather was also part of the 'look'.

Jerry Hopkins in his biography *Elvis* (Simon and Schuster, 1971) described the magic of an Elvis performance:
'He looked at the girls in the front row with lidded eyes. . . . During the song's instrumental break he gave them that lopsided grin and maybe twitched one leg. . . . The next song might be a rocker, giving Elvis a chance to show the folks what they'd come for. Now both legs were twitching – jerking and snapping back into that original braced position. . .'

Presley made his first of many movies in 1957. Commercial firms begged for licences to use his name and face on products – everything from socks and charm bracelets to diaries and mirrors.

Karen Moline was a fan who wrote an open 'letter to Elvis':
'. . . I'm just one of the millions, the fans, the expectant sobbing, screaming mass. . . . You'd flash us that special, steamy pouty grin, swiveling those hips in our direction. . .'.

Another fan, Gay McRae, wrote:
'Once Elvis touched your life, it seemed he touched your very soul. That's why people didn't just 'like' Elvis; when they said they *loved* him, it's because they really did.'

joins the Army

Rock 'n' roll era

ELVIS was 'The King' of a distinctive new type of pop music which emerged in the 1950s. Small groups used electronically amplified instruments and simple harmonies fusing Gospel, Jazz, Rhythm and Blues, Country, Boogie and the music of Southern Blacks. The term 'rock 'n' roll' was first used by an American broadcaster Alan Freed who in 1951 hosted an R & B record show entitled 'Moondog's Rock 'n' Roll Party'. He probably took this from an old blues song called 'My Baby Rocks me with a Steady Roll'.

The first American rock 'n' roll hit was 'Sh-boom' which was first sung in 1954. In 1955 it entered the music charts in a version by a group known as the Crewcuts. The first world-wide rock 'n' roll hit was 'Rock Around the Clock' by Bill Haley and his Comets in 1955. They had first reached the charts in America and Britain in 1954 with 'Shake, Rattle and Roll'. Elvis first hit the number one spot in Britain in 1957 with 'All Shook Up'. His total of number one records in Britain is matched only by the Beatles.

There were many other great names in 1950s music. Chuck Berry made his first recording, 'Maybellene', in 1955 and it sold over a million copies. Connie Francis had many hits after 'Who's Sorry Now' in 1958.

Lonnie Donegan, a British 1950s star, had a hit with 'Rock Island Line', which became popular in the American charts as well. Britain's first rock 'n' roll band was Tony Crombie and his Rockets who entered the British charts in 1956 with 'Teach You to Rock'. Britain's first rock 'n' roll star was Tommy Steele whose 'Rock with the Cavern' entered the charts in 1956. His first number one hit was 'Singing the

Teenagers at a UK secondary school jive at an evening dance. Girls wore white ankle socks and full skirts. Male trousers were loose with turn-up cuffs.

Blues' later the same year. Cliff Richard's first entry in the UK charts was 'Move It' in 1958. This was followed by many other hits.

In the 1960s the term 'rock' replaced 'rock 'n' roll' – but the music of the 1950s had much influence and remains popular today.

Teddy boys

THE BRITISH version of rebellious American 'hoods' were the 'teddy boys'. In the early 1950s these adopted an Edwardian style of dress, with drainpipe trousers, drape jackets, slim-jim ties, shoes with thick crêpe soles and greasy hair styles. The style was first started in the late 1940s by the *Tailor and Cutter* magazine. It was dropped by the fashionable when it became taken up by young street 'roughs'.

World News

De Gaulle elected President

THERE WAS SOME political chaos in France after the Second World War with no party having a majority in the National Assembly. A report came out in 1958 saying that France was to grant independence to Algeria. This led to riots by French people in Algiers and the collapse of the French government. General Charles de Gaulle (1890-1970) had been the wartime leader of the Free French. The election in November 1958 brought him out of retirement and into office as the country's new President of the Fifth Republic. De Gaulle negotiated the French withdrawal from Algeria and emphasized the importance of new links between France and the African people. He was given wider powers than any President in the Third or Fourth republics and was later re-elected in 1965.

The referendum that brought De Gaulle into office also included voting by France's black African territories. All except Guinea voted against complete independence. In November/December, Chad, Congo, Gabon, Mali, Mauritania, Senegal, Ivory Coast, Niger, Central Africa, Upper Volta and Dahomey became republics in the French Union.

General de Gaulle is shown speaking in 1958, saying he is ready to lead the French Republic. A famous quote from the General in 1958 was 'How can you govern a country which produces 265 different kinds of cheese?'

Notting Hill race riot

AN EXPLOSIVE RACE RIOT took place in the Notting Hill area of London in September. Petrol bombs and thousands of milk bottles were thrown as police tried to control the crowds. The trouble began as a gang of white youth demonstrated outside a house occupied by black people.

Fisheries war

IN AUGUST the Icelandic government unilaterally declared a 12-mile (19-km) fishing limit. This was to stop foreign boats fishing close to Iceland's shores. In September British trawlers began defying the 12-mile limit and a fisheries war began.

Last debutantes

DÉBUTANTES were presented at Buckingham Palace for the very last time in March 1958. It had been the tradition for daughters of the aristocracy and prominent people to be presented at court.

CND begins

THE CAMPAIGN FOR NUCLEAR DISARMAMENT began in London in 1958. James Cameron, journalist and author, was a founding member and recalled the beginning:

In late 1957 a movement was growing that denounced the nuclear weapon as the symbol of contemporary folly. . . . It took many forms, coalescing for a while in the organisation with the jaw-breaking title of the National Campaign Against Nuclear Weapons Tests (NCANWT). . . . Then at the beginning of 1958, there took place a meeting at the home of John Collins, canon of St Pauls . . . on that evening was born the Campaign for Nuclear Disarmament. A great number of people was present . . . I seem to recall Bertrand Russell, J.B. Priestley . . . Ritchie Calder, Kingsley Martin, A.J.P. Taylor. . . . So CND came into being, under the presidency of Lord Russell and the chairmanship of John Collins. . . .

Our first task was to let the country know of our existence, The campaign took over the Central Hall, Westminster, for an inaugural meeting on 17 February. It was an extraordinary success, transcending anything any of us had believed possible. More than two thousand people jammed the hall, four overflow halls were packed. . . . The CND people, like all rational human beings, saw total international nuclear disarmament as the principal chance for any final salvation of the species . . . Easter of 1958 saw the first Aldermaston march. . . . It was an uncommonly disagreeable experience in the physical sense – a four-day trudge of 50 miles from the Atomic Weapons Research Establishment in Berkshire to London – but it was for me the one emotionally stimulating experience of the year . . . this annual ritual attracted the derision of the Press, which concentrated its ridicule on the outstanding eccentric who were always prominent, the bearded and tousled nonconformists with the guitars, ignoring the long and patient tramping columns of wholly normal and unremarkable housewives and workers and shopkeepers and clerks. . .

James Cameron, *Point of Departure*, Arthur Barker, 1968.

First UK motorway

BRITAIN'S first stretch of motorway was opened by Prime Minister Harold Macmillan in December. He declared the eight mile Preston by-pass in Lancashire 'a token of what was to follow'.

First parking metres

IT WAS ANNOUNCED in February that Britain's first parking metres were to be installed in Mayfair, London in July. This was also the year when UK motorists received their first parking tickets, in March.

Dr Kwame Nkrumah, Prime Minister of Ghana.

All-African People's Conference

AN 'All-African People's Conference' of 200 representatives of 50 African political parties, trade unions and organizations met in December in Accra, Ghana. The main purpose was 'to formulate concrete plans and work out the tactics and strategy of the African non-violent revolution'. Africans wanted to speed-up the liberation of colonies into independent states.

Dr Nkrumah, Prime Minister of Ghana, promised support from his country. 'Our struggle is to wipe out imperialism and colonialism from this continent and to erect in their place a union of free, independent African states . . .' He described as 'imperialist fiction' the idea that Africa had made no contribution to civilization. Nkrumah recalled that great empires had existed on the African continent in past centuries.

There was some controversy at the conference on whether violent methods should be used for liberation. Dr Fanon Omar of Algeria said: '. . . all forms of struggle must be adopted . . . and not excluding violence.' Among the resolutions passed at the conference was one to the UN requesting all colonial powers to withdraw from Africa. It was decided to set up a secretariat in Accra to co-ordinate political activities of anti-colonial forces in Africa.

Sport and the Arts

Tin Drum a sensation

'FEARFUL and wonderful – horribly brilliant.'

'An extraordinary novel . . . original, violent, raucous and funny.'

The reviews of Günter Grass's new novel *The Tin Drum* praised its black humour and social analysis. Grass, born in Germany in 1927, grew up as a member of the Hitler Youth. He was a soldier, jazz musician and sculptor as well as a writer. *The Tin Drum* is a satirical look at the Hitler years with the central character stunted – both physically and mentally. Oskar deliberately stopped growing at the age of three. The title comes from Oskar's childhood obsession. He recalls: 'In that period, roughly between the ages of seven and ten, I went through a drum in two weeks flat. From ten to fourteen I demolished an instrument in less than a week. . .'. At the end of the book, Oskar is to be discharged from a mental hospital after his 30th birthday; but he is 'still afraid of the Black Witch': 'Always somewhere behind me, the Black Witch / Now ahead of me too, facing me, Black. . .'

Dr Zhivago published

BORIS PASTERNAK was a well-known poet and translator in the USSR. His first novel caused a sensation and even resulted in his expulsion from the Writers' Union. The Russians refused to publish *Dr Zhivago* saying it showed 'non-acceptance of the social revolution' that had taken place there. *Dr Zhivago* is the study of the gradual decline of an idealistic intellectual who had welcomed the revolution then been disillusioned. The book was first published in Italy in 1957. Pasternak was offered the Nobel Prize for Literature in 1958 but felt he had to refuse because there was so much hostility to the novel in Russia.

Despite his disenchantment, Pasternak was loyal to his country. In 1958 he wrote to the Russian leader Khrushchev saying 'departure beyond the borders of my country is for me equivalent to death.' On the Nobel Prize, Pasternak said:

I am caught like a beast at bay, / Somewhere are people, freedom, light, / But all I hear is the baying of the pack, / There is no way out for me.

Team wiped out

SEVEN Manchester United football players were killed in an air crash on their return from a match against Red Star Belgrade.

Guggenheim finished

FRANK LLOYD WRIGHT (1869-1959) was one of the great architects of the twentieth century. He was part of the modern 'functionalist' school which said the design of a structure was determined by what would go inside it. A building should 'express' its function. The clean horizontal lines and open spaces of his buildings revolutionized architectural styles.

Wright's Guggenheim Museum of Modern Art in New York was finished in 1958. It has a winding circular form, allowing visitors to move in a continuous way from one exhibition to another. Wright believed a building should be part of the site. 'No house should ever be *on* any hill or on anything. It should be *of* the hill, belonging to it, so hill and house could live together each the happier for the other.'

Frank Lloyd Wright's Guggenheim Museum in New York City.

Non-stick pans

A FRENCH engineer Mark Grégoire made the first non-stick frying pans in 1958 with the brand name 'Tefal'. These used a coating made of PTFE (polytetrafluoroethylene) which was unaffected by chemicals, moisture, sunlight or heat between –260°C and 330°C. Not even chewing gum would stick to it. PTFE had been discovered accidentally in 1938 by an industrial chemist in Delaware. At first it was used for handling corrosive chemicals and later for heat protection of rockets and missiles. Its use for non-stick cookware remains very popular.

Stereo records

STEREOPHONIC RECORDS were first issued in 1958 by Audio Fidelity in the US, Pye in Britain and closely followed by Decca. The systems were made possible by improvements such as better styluses to pick up the stereo signals in the groove.

Squirrel monkey dies

A SOUTH AMERICAN squirrel monkey survived a 15 minute ride in the nose cone of a US Army Jupiter missile but the animal died because ships in the South Atlantic could not recover the capsule.

Integrated circuit invented

THE INTEGRATED CIRCUIT was invented in the US, much reducing the cost of computer operations. The circuit also increased the speed by which calculations could be made.

Explorers and SCORE launched

ON 31 JANUARY a Jupiter C rocket put Explorer I (the first US artificial satellite) into space. Explorer I was an 18-pound (8.2-kg) satellite which took 115 minutes to orbit the earth. The satellite revealed the presence of a cloak of radiation held around the earth by its magnetic field. This was called the Van Allen belt after the man who identified it, and was the first major scientific discovery resulting from the space race. More satellites followed. In July, the US Army successfully launched Explorer IV.

By December 1958, the US was experimenting with communications satellites. In the week before Christmas, a satellite called SCORE (Signal Communication by Orbiting Relay Equipment) was launched, It carried pre-recorded messages from President Eisenhower giving Christmas greetings to the American people, broadcast automatically from space. Other messages were also transmitted for a total of 13 days.

SCORE was drawn back to earth and burned up in the earth's atmosphere towards the end of January 1959. It had been in orbit for more than a month. SCORE proved that intelligible messages could be received from space.

Diagram of the Jupiter C rocket that launched Explorer 1, America's first satellite, into orbit from Cape Canaveral Missile Base. Instruments packed into the satellite sent back data via radio.

NASA created

US PRESIDENT EISENHOWER signed a bill in July creating NASA, the National Aeronautics and Space Administration. In September NASA announced its space programme, including plans for a manned earth satellite within two years, landing a man on the moon within 6-10 years, and exploration of Mars in 10-15 years.

Strontium 90 increase

SCIENTISTS from America's Columbia University reported that nuclear explosions during the previous year had increased by one-third the concentration of radioactive strontium 90 in human bodies.

Some firsts . . .

THE FIRST transatlantic commercial jet service (British)
The first intercontinental ballistic missile, ICBM (Russian)

1959 Cuba – Castro

Cuba's revolution

THE DICTATORSHIP of President Batista of Cuba collapsed on 1 January 1959 and he fled to the Dominican Republic. Forces led by Fidel Castro had taken control of nearly the whole of the Eastern part of the island. Dr Castro entered Havana, the Cuban capital, in triumph. Crowds welcomed him enthusiastically and he was given 21-gun salutes. 'Havana goes wild' read the headline in the *Daily Express*. On 16 February, Castro was sworn in as Cuban Prime Minister.

Castro's rise to power

FIDEL CASTRO was a 32 year-old lawyer at the time he became leader. He had worked for over five years to overthrow the Batista regime, building up a strong guerrilla army in the mountains. The son of a wealthy sugar planter, Castro hated the corruption of the rich and the Bastista government.

Fidel and his brother Raul began their anti-Batista campaign on 26 July 1953 with an attack on army barracks. (26 July is now celebrated as a national holiday in Cuba.) Over the next few years, he was imprisoned and then went into exile in the US and Mexico. It was in Mexico that Ernesto 'Che' Guevara joined Castro's movement. Part of the reason why Castro's efforts finally succeeded were described by *The Times* correspondent in Havana at the start of 1959:

Last year, when rebel activities were intensified and the Batista regime reacted with increasing ruthlessness, support of the rebels increased . . . the Fidel Castro revolt only really gained impetus when more moderate Opposition leaders had failed in their efforts to persuade General Batista to exercise restraint and reinstate the constitutional government he alone promised. . . .

During late 1957 and early 1958 Castro's guerrilla forces wrecked warehouses and machinery and burned large amounts of sugar in their raids on sugar plantations. The strategy was to weaken the government economically by hurting sugar production, which accounted for a third of Cuba's national income. In March 1958, Castro issued a manifesto to the Cuban people declaring 'total war on the Batista tyranny'. He called on the armed forces and the general population to join the movement. He warned that all transport and communications would be brought to a standstill throughout eastern Cuba by guerrilla attacks.

Following the call for a general strike on 9 April 1958, there was violent street fighting in Havana. Young men seized temporary control of the radio and television stations and gun battles were fought. By autumn 1958, Castro's forces had gained control of nearly the whole of Oriente province and had started their westward march of liberation.

The new government

CASTRO'S new government took drastic measures to stop graft and corruption, especially in gambling casinos. Even the traditional lottery was stopped. Another change was to cancel government subsidies paid to Cuban newspapers and magazines.

In May 1959, the Cuban government approved a far-reaching land reform law. One main provision was that no person or company could own more than 1000 acres (405 ha.) of land in Cuba, with the exception of some land used for sugar-growing, rice-growing or cattle ranching. Where properties exceeded 1000 acres, the land above the limit was to be redistributed to landless peasants. A National Institute of Agrarian Reform, headed by Dr Castro, would decide which lands were to be expropriated and redistributed. The law led to the expropriation of American-owned sugar mills and plantations in Cuba, accounting for 40 per cent of Cuba's sugar production. The US government sent a note to Cuba on 11 June expressing 'serious concern' for the inadequate compensation being offered. The Cuban government replied on 15 June, saying that it alone had the power to decide what was in the best interests of the Cuban people.

Fidel Castro (left) is shown shaking hands with Mayor Wagner of New York City.

in Power

Relations with America

THE UNITED STATES at first welcomed Castro's government but was upset by the execution of some 200 'war criminals' accused by Castro of killing pro-Castro rebels. Castro visited the US in April of 1959, saying he was in search of 'good relations and good economic understanding'. He declared he was a democrat and strongly denied suggestions that he was a 'dictator'. Castro said the revolution was misunderstood abroad. Its sole aim was to abolish poverty, injustice and unemployment and help the Cuban people build their economic base so all would have 'the right to live, to eat and to work'. He expressed opposition to Communism ('which flourishes on empty bellies'). Castro said it would have little chance of success in Cuba if people had enough to eat, the chance to work and a soundly based economy.

America was unhappy with Cuba's land reforms in May which affected US business interests. In 1960 the US Congress reduced Cuba's sugar quota by 95 per cent which greatly reduced Cuba's largest single market for its single largest product. In 1961 the US broke off diplomatic relations and Castro developed close links with the USSR. The first trade-and-aid agreements between Cuba and Russia started in 1960 and over the next few years Cuba's friendliness to the USSR was a great source of concern to America. In the early 1960s the US and Russia came close to war over the placing of Soviet missiles in Cuba, only 150 km from American soil.

Treaty on Antarctica

A 12-NATION conference on peaceful international scientific co-operation in Antarctica was held in Washington DC in October/November. This resulted in a 30-year treaty agreeing to the free use of the Antarctic continent for peaceful scientific purposes. There was also a ban on all military activities in the area and the world's first international inspection system was set up to enforce this.

At the signing ceremony on 1 December President Eisenhower described the treaty as 'an inspiring example of what can be achieved by international co-operation in the field of science and in the pursuit of peace'.

Prime Minister Harold Macmillan is shown speaking on a pre-election tour of the country.

UK general election

ON 8 SEPTEMBER the UK Prime Minister Harold Macmillan announced a dissolution of Parliament and that a General Election would be held on 8 October. This resulted in the return to power of the Conservative Government with an increased overall majority. The Conservatives had won three General Elections in the 1950s (1951, 1955, and 1959) and increased their majority each time. Macmillan broadcast a statement to the nation on 9 October:

. . . 'My colleagues and I are deeply grateful for the confidence which has been shown in us. . . . This election has shown that the class war is obsolete. . .'. Hugh Gaitskell conceded defeat for the Labour Party but said: 'After the setback we still represent half the nation. . . . We shall attack again and again and again until we win. . .'. The Liberal Party came third but increased its poll. Their leader Jo Grimmond commented: 'I have been saying for a long time that what is wanted is a new Radical Party to take the place of the Socialist Party as an alternative to Conservatism.'

The three party election manifestos included the following:

Conservative: . . . two out of three families in the country now own television, one in three has a car or motor cycle, twice as many are taking holidays away from home – these are welcome signs of the increasing enjoyment of leisure. . . .

Labour: . . . One of the greatest barriers to equality of opportunity in our schools is the segregation of our children into grammar and other types of schools at age 11. This is why we shall get rid of the 11-plus examination. . .

Liberal: . . . the poverty of the pensioner shames our wealth. Raise the pension to £3 for a single person and £4 16s for a married couple . . . Liberals would give Wales and Scotland Parliaments of their own. . .

Archbishop Makarios of Cyprus (1913-77).

Law of the Sea conference fails

THE SECOND UN Conference on the Law of the Sea took place in Geneva in March/April with delegates from 88 countries. The conference was concerned with two questions which the first UN Conference in 1958 had failed to resolve: (1) the width of the territorial sea (2) the breadth of zone in which coastal states could exercise exclusive fishing rights.

No agreement was reached on these points in 1959 and the UK Minister of Agriculture and Fisheries described this as a 'bitter disappointment'. The only proposal approved by the conference was a resolution sponsored by Ethiopia, Ghana and Liberia calling for technical aid to poorer countries for their fishing industries.

Cyprus independent

IN FEBRUARY, leaders of Britain, Greece, Turkey and Cyprus met in London and agreed the basis for establishing Cyprus as an independent republic. There was much conflict between the Greeks and Turks over the island. The Turkish Foreign Minister said:

. . . We are meeting today to achieve the solution of an intricate problem of diplomacy and foreign policy . . . Everybody knows how full of difficulties the task has been. . .

Archbishop Makarios spoke as a representative of the Greek-Cypriot community:

A new era opens today for the people of Cyprus . . . the two communities will be able to develop the welfare of the Island to their common benefit.

Makarios was elected first President of the republic in December elections.

Riots in Léopoldville

RIOTING broke out in Léopoldville, in the Belgian Congo, in January and February 1959. Africans in the colony wanted self-government. Widespread unemployment amongst blacks and the sharp differences in living standards between whites and blacks added to the anti-European feeling. The Belgian government finally announced on 13 January its decision to grant independence to the Congo in a series of gradual stages.

Steel strike

NEGOTIATIONS for a new labour contract in the US steel industry broke down and a strike began on 15 July affecting most of production. In October, the US Government obtained a Court injunction requiring the steel plants to resume work for a 'cooling-off' period of 80 days. The union appealed against this but the plants reopened in November and two months later a settlement was finally reached. The 116-day shut-down was the longest ever in the US steel industry and had effects on all parts of the American economy. It was estimated that 37 per cent of all manufacturing jobs in the USA were dependent on the steel industry.

In brief . . .

– ALASKA and Hawaii became the 49th and 50th states of America.
– Oklahoma repealed prohibition. This left Mississippi as the only 'dry' state in America, the only state where alcoholic beverages could not be sold.

Sport and the Arts

'New wave' films

ALAIN RESNAIS'S film *Hirshima Mon Amour* appeared in 1959. This examined the effects of war on human relationships and was one of the Nouvelle Vague (New Wave) films produced in the 1950s and 60s. This term was used to describe the exploratory film work of young French directors such as François Truffaut, Jean-Luc Godard and Louis Malle. Truffaut's *The 400 Blows* also appeared in 1959. It showed the New Wave trend for fast, low-budget productions with a loose, improvisational style.

Premieres

LORRAINE HANSBERRY'S play *A Raisin in the Sun* opened on Broadway, telling the story of an American black family trying to raise itself out of a slum environment.
Gypsy (the musical based on the life of Gypsy Rose Lee)
Some Like it Hot (the comic film starring Marilyn Monroe, Jack Lemmon and Tony Curtis)
The Mouse that Roared (film starring Peter Sellers playing a number of roles)
The Sound of Music (Rogers and Hammerstein musical starring Mary Martin and Theodore Bikel)
Ben-Hur (epic film starring Charlton Heston)
On the Beach (film starring Gregory Peck, Ava Gardner and Fred Astaire)
Sweet Bird of Youth (play by Tennessee Williams)

Brazilian at Wimbledon

MARIA ESTHER BUENO won the women's singles title at Wimbledon in 1959 beating Darlene Hard of the US.

Stockhausen's Groups

GERMAN COMPOSER Karlheinz Stockhausen produced one of his most exciting works 'Groups' in 1959. It is performed simultaneously by three orchestras in three separate parts of a concert hall. Stockhausen said of this work:

They play . . . partially independently in different tempi; from time to time they meet in common rhythm; they call to each other and answer each other; for a whole period of time one hears only music from the left, or from the front, or from the right. The sound wanders from one orchestra to another.

This is an example of spatial or directional music. Unlike traditional performances, spatial music comes to the listener from several directions.

Stockhausen was one of a growing number of composers interested in electronic music in the 1950s. Besides composing, he did what he could to promote the style. Stockhausen developed a system of notation for electronic sounds and in 1955 helped to found *Die Reihe* ('The Row'), a music journal for which he wrote about electronic music.

Truly the music of the space age, Stockhausen's work seems to be reaching out. He once said:

My music must receive those universal vibrations like some fantastic radio . . . I believe the moment has come in the Western Hemisphere to move from intelligence to intuition, to the irrational, where spirit replaces flesh.

The 1959 painting Pompeii by Hans Hofmann was typical of the Abstract Expressionism which dominated art in the decade.

Electronic synthesizer

A 'SYNTHESIZER' is an electronic instrument which allows musicians to make new sounds as well as imitate sounds of conventional instruments. Technicians at the Radio Corporation of America devised a synthesizer in 1959 that produced various sounds according to instructions on perforated tapes. Simple wave forms are generated electronically and then changed into the organized sound we know as music. The product is usually recorded on magnetic tape and can be edited as wanted.

Zarchin process

AN AGREEMENT was signed in Israel in December forming a joint US-Israel company to convert sea water into fresh water. The method of desalination was discovered by a Russian-born Israeli scientist, Dr Alexander Zarchin. The process was based on the continuous freezing and subsequent melting of sea water to free it of salt.

Zarchin's discovery was hailed as a 'great scientific breakthrough'. The president of the Chicago corporation in water-supply who signed the agreement said it would allow desalination of water at a cost comparable with the average cost of water in the USA. He added that construction of the first industrial desalination plant in Israel would begin in 1960. A second plant would be built in the south-west USA. It was hoped that conversion plants with a capacity of a billion gallons of fresh water a day would be operating in various parts of the world by 1965. The discovery would be of major importance in arid areas, such as the Negev in Israel, where lack of water was an obstacle to development.

Fast breeder reactor

THE FIRST fast breeder reactor to generate electricity successfully was in operation at Dounreay on the coast at Caithness, Scotland in 1959. Dounreay Fast Reactor and other fast breeders have the advantage of being able to convert uranium-238 into fissile plutonium-239 at a rapid rate. This means that 50 to 60 times more energy can be drawn from the world's uranium.

Mini atomic generation

A MINIATURE atomic generator weighing only five pounds was announced in the USA in January. The device was acclaimed as a 'significant breakthrough in the direct conversion of heat into electrical energy'. It was important as a light, compact power source for instruments carried in earth satellites. Known as SNAP III, the device was a mere 4¾ inches (12 cm) in diameter and 5½ inches (14 cm) high.

The new Hovercraft in action.

Hovercraft flight

COWES, Isle of Wight was the site of the first hovercraft flight, in 1959. The four-tonne Saunders-Roe SR-NI was soon able to reach 68 knots. Christopher Cockerell invented the hovercraft as a means of crossing water, marsh or flatland. The craft is easy to manoeuvre as it floats on a cushion of air.

In brief. . .

– THE WORLD'S first nuclear-powered merchant ship was launched in the US
– US launched the Vanguard satellite, the first weather station in space

Time Chart

World News	Sport and the Arts	Science and Technology

1950
(January) End of milk rationing in UK.
(January) US confirms production of hydrogen bomb.
(February) Clement Atlee re-elected PM in Britain.
(February) Grave famine reported in China.
(April) Delhi Pact signed.
(April) Anti-Communist 'Loyalty Day' parades in US.
(June) North Korea invades South Korea.
US Senator McCarthy charges that State Department is full of Communists.

(August) Florence Chadwick swims English Channel in new record speed.
The Bald Soprano play produced.
Bertrand Russell wins Nobel Prize.
England enters World Cup soccer contest for first time.

Continuous casting of steel introduced.
First UNIVAC computers produced.
First reports linking smoking to lung cancer.
Diners' Club credit card begins.
New element, californium.
First human kidney transplant.
First concentrated milk.

1951
(February) Iron and steel nationalized in UK.
(March) Group Areas Act in South Africa.
(May) Festival of Britain opens.
(July) India starts family planning campaign.
(August) McCarran charges there are three to five million subversive aliens in US.
Burgess and Maclean defect to USSR.
(October) Winston Churchill wins General Election in UK.
(November) Peron re-elected President in Argentina.

Catcher in the Rye published.
Parachuting a recognized sport.
Cage's *Music for Changes* first performed.
The King and I first performed.
The Caine Mutiny published.

First colour TV, in US.
New progestin discovered leading to birth control pill.
World's first atomic heating plant.

1952
(March) UN Commission on Status of Women approves draft convention.
(July) King Farouk abdicates.
(September) Mau Mau raiders attack.
(December) Indonesia joins Colombo Plan.
McCarran-Walter Immigration law passed in US.

The African Queen film released.
High Noon voted best film.
Limelight film released.
The Old Man and the Sea novel published.
East of Eden novel published.

First hydrogen bomb tested.
Cinemascope introduced.
First heart-pacemaker.
First commercial jet service.
First transistor hearing aid.
First tranquillizer marketed.

1953
Eisenhower begins as US President.
(February) Sweet rationing ends in UK.
Stalin dies.
Hillary climbs Mt Everest.
Queen Elizabeth II crowned.
US creates Department of Health, Education and Welfare.
Rosenbergs executed.
IPPF established.

The Crucible play opens.
Zorba the Greek novel published.
Go Tell it on the Mountain novel published.

First heart-lung machine.
Patent on soya as meat substitute.
Kinsey Report published on sexual behaviour.
Piltdown Man found to be a hoax.
DNA structure revealed.

1954
(March) 10th conference of Organization of American States.
(May) US Supreme Court rules segregation in schools unconstitutional.
(June) Nkrumah elected head of Gold Coast.
(September) First National Health Service Health Centre in Britain.
(December) Britain signs treaty with European Coal and Steel Community.
Dien Bien Phu battle in Vietnam.

Lord of the Flies novel published.
Roger Bannister runs mile in less than four minutes.
A Star is Born film released.
On the Waterfront film released.
Under Milk Wood play performed.
Henri Matisse dies.

First mass polio vaccines given.
First nuclear reactor to generate electricity.
First transistor radio.
IBM mechanical translator machine.
First Eurovision TV programme.

Time Chart

World News	Sport and the Arts	Science and Technology

1955

(April) Anthony Eden becomes PM of Britain.
(May) US Supreme Court directs states to desegregate schools.
Civil rights boycott of buses in Montgomery, Alabama.
US Supreme Court rulings for desegregation of some public places.
International Atomic Energy Agency created by UN.
International Coffee Bureau starts.
Burgess-Maclean-Philby spy debate.

Lolita novel published.
Rebel Without a Cause film released.
Davy Crockett film opens.
Lady and the Tramp film released.

First nuclear-powered submarine.
First application of fibre optics.
Plans revealed for International Geophysical Year July 1957–December 1958.
First solar-powered hot-water system built.

1956

(January) Sudan becomes independent republic.
(January) New railway links China and Russia.
(February) Khrushchev denounces Stalin.
(March) Tunisia and Morocco become independent countries.
(July) IFC formed by World Bank.
Hungarian Revolution.
Suez Crisis.

Look Back in Anger play first performed.
English version of *Waiting for Godot* play published.
Rocky Marciano retires.
The King and I film released.
Around the World in 80 Days film released.
Lady Sings the Blues biography published.
Compulsion published.

First practical videotape recorder for television pictures.
First large-scale nuclear power plant, Calder Hall.
First telephone transmitting pictures as well as sound.
First synthetic diamonds.

1957

Sputniks I and II launched.
Vanguard satellite fails.
EEC established.
Little Rock Arkansas civil rights struggle in US.
Malaya independent.
First BBC Schools television broadcast.
UK Clean Air Act.
Eisenhower Doctrine on Middle East.
Home Guard Disbanded.

The Birthday Party play produced.
Albert Camus wins Nobel Prize.
'Sack' and 'trapeze' dresses.
Built-up shoe in high-jumping.
West Side Story musical opens.
On the Road published

First Pressurized Water Reactor (PWR).
Windscale nuclear reactor overheats.
First portable electric typewriter.
Borazon discovered.

1958

(November) De Gaulle elected French president.
(December) All-African People's Conference.
Elvis drafted into US Army.
Campaign for Nuclear Disarmament begins.
Britain–Iceland Fisheries war begins.
First UK motorway.
Notting Hill race riot in UK.

The Tin Drum novel published.
Guggenheim Museum completed.
Pasternak offered Nobel Prize for *Dr Zhivago* novel.
Parachuting a recognized sport.
Cage's *Music for Changes* first performed.
The King and I first performed.
The Caine Mutiny published.

First non-stick frying pans.
First stereophonic records issued.
Explorer I into space.
NASA created in US.
Integrated circuit invented.
First transatlantic commercial jet service.
First intercontinental ballistic missile (ICBM).

1959

(March/April) Law of the Sea Conference.
(October) Macmillan re-elected.
(October/November) Treaty on Antarctica.
Castro takes power in Cuba.
Cyprus independent.
Belgium announces Congo will be independent.
Alaska and Hawaii become 49th and 50th US states.

'New wave' films.
Stockhausen's *Groups* composition produced.
Some Like it Hot film released.
The Mouse That Roared film released.
Ben Hur film released.
On the Road novel published.
Sweet Bird of Youth play published.

First electronic synthesizer.
First fast breeder reactor generates electricity successfully.
First hovercraft flight.
Miniature atomic generator announced.

Key figures of the decade

Fidel Castro (1926-   )

CASTRO was the son of a successful Cuban sugar planter and decided to study law. He fought cases on behalf of the poor and battled against official corruption in the Batista regime. In 1953, Fidel and his brother Raul led an unsuccessful uprising against the government. Fidel was sentenced to 15 years in prison but was released within a year and fled to the USA and Mexico. In December 1958, Fidel led a full-scale attack which forced Batista to flee Cuba. Castro became Cuba's leader in February 1959, proclaiming his government Marxist-Leninist and developing close links with the USSR. He began large reforms in farming and industry.

Winston Churchill (1874-1965)

THIS GREAT British statesman and author entered the House of Commons as an MP in 1901 and held various government offices. Churchill became Prime Minister on 10 May 1940, the day that Hitler invaded Holland. Having led Britain through the war, he announced victory in 1945 and won the cheers of the nation. However, he lost the General Election and only became Prime Minister again in 1951, at the age of 77. Churchill served as PM until 1955 and had a world reputation as leader and orator. In his later years he was described as the 'greatest living Englishman'.

Charles de Gaulle (1890-1970)

WHEN FRANCE FELL to the Germans in 1940, General de Gaulle fled to England to raise the standard of the 'Free French'. At the time of liberation in 1944, it was de Gaulle who led one of the first forces to enter Paris. He was elected first President of the Fifth Republic in 1958, and served from 1959 to 1969. De Gaulle's foreign policy included granting independence to all French African colonies.

Sir Anthony Eden (1897-1977)

HAVING BECOME a British MP in 1923, Eden went on to serve in a number of government posts. He was secretary of state for the dominions in 1939-40 and war secretary in 1940. It was Eden's appeal that started the Home Guard. Eden became secretary of state for foreign affairs 1940-45 and again from 1951 to 1955. He was Prime Minister from 1955 to 1957, when he resigned mainly for health reasons. It was Eden who in 1956 ordered British and French forces to occupy the Suez Canal Zone ahead of the invading Israeli army. His action was condemned by the United Nations and brought mixed reactions in Britain.

Dwight David Eisenhower (1890-1969)

BORN IN TEXAS, USA, Eisenhower followed a military career. In 1942 he became US commander of allied forces for the descent on North Africa. In 1944, he was the top commander of the D-Day cross-channel invasion of the European mainland from Britain. Eisenhower was made supreme commander of NATO forces in 1950 and stood as Republican candidate in the 1952 US Presidential election. He won and served as the 34th American president from 1953 to 1961.

Nikita Sergeyevich Khrushchev (1894-1971)

KHRUSHCHEV began life as a Russian shepherd boy and locksmith, and could hardly read or write until the age of 25. He joined the Communist Party in 1918 and rose rapidly within the organization. On the death of Stalin in 1953, Khrushchev became first secretary of the All Union Party. At the 20th Congress of the Communist Party in 1956 he denounced Stalin. Before being deposed in 1964 Khrushchev did much to further Soviet ambitions abroad.

Harold Macmillan (1894-1986)

THIS BRITISH PUBLISHER and politician first became an MP in 1924. He remained a backbencher until 1940 when Churchill made him parliamentary under secretary to the Ministry of Supply. Macmillan was Minister of Housing 1951-4, Minister of Defence 1954-5, and Chancellor of the Exchequer 1955-7. He served as Prime Minister from 1957 to 1963. His 'wind of change' speech in 1960 acknowledged the inevitability of African independence. Several setbacks in the early 1960s and especially the Profumo scandal in 1963 led to his leaving office.

Key figures of the decade

Gamal Abdul Nasser (1918-1970)

AS AN EGYPTIAN ARMY OFFICER, Nasser was unhappy with the corruption of the Farouk regime. Nasser headed a military Junta which brought the downfall of the king. Nasser then became president of Egypt 1956-8 and of the United Arab Republic (UAR) 1958-70. The UAR was formed by a federation with Syria and was part of Nasser's overall aim for an empire across North Africa. Syria later withdrew from the UAR and there were other set-backs to his plans. After the six day Arab – Israeli war in 1967, heavy losses on the Arab side prompted Nasser to resign, but he was persuaded to change his mind.

Shri Jawaharlal Nehru (1889-1964)

EDUCATED IN ENGLAND, Nehru returned to his native India in 1912. In 1919 he joined Gandhi's movement against colonial rule. Nehru spent five and a half years in gaol for his Nationalist activities. After Indian independence, Nehru became the first Prime Minister of India 1950-66. He followed a neutral policy during the Cold War and often acted as a go-between for the Superpowers. Nehru's daughter Indira succeeded him as Prime Minister in 1966.

Kwame Nkrumah (1909-1972)

EDUCATED IN AMERICA and then in England, Nkrumah returned to Africa in 1949 and formed a nationalist Convention People's party. The slogan was 'self government now'. In 1950 Nhrumah was put in prison for calling strikes but was released a year later. He became known as the 'Ghandhi of Africa', being a main leader in the struggle against white colonial rule. Nkrumah became the first Prime Minister of the independent state of Ghana (1957-60) and then president (1960-66) when Ghana became a republic. In 1966 his regime was toppled by a military coup while Nkrumah was in China.

Juan Peron (1895-1974)

PERON WAS AN ARGENTINE POLITICIAN who first served as minister of war and secretary of labor. He was Vice-President in 1944-5 and was then President 1946-55. Peron was very popular amongst the masses because of his drive for social reforms. However, in 1955 he lost much support and was deposed. Peron became President again in 1973 with his second wife as Vice-President. His first wife Eva had died in 1952 at the age of 33. She had been a powerful influence, campaigning for changes such as the right of women to vote. She founded the Eva Peron Foundation to promote social welfare.

Mao Zedong (Mao Tse-tung) (1893-1976)

MAO ZEDONG led the Chinese Revolution and founded the new People's Republic of China in 1949. He wanted social reforms to distribute wealth more equally. He also wanted to change China into a modern industrial state. China changed dramatically in the 1950s and Chairman Mao continued to lead his country until his death.

Books for further reading

C.J. Bartlett, *A History of Post-War Britain, 1945-1974*, Longman, 1977

Trevor Cairns, *The Twentieth Century*, Cambridge University Press, 1983

Derek Heater, *Our World This Century*, Oxford University Press, 1982

C.R. Hill, *Growing up in the 1950s*, Batsford, 1983

Colin MacInnes, *England, Half English*, A portrait of London in the 1950s, Hogarth Press, 1986

P.J. Madjwick and others, *Britain Since 1945*, Hutchinson, 1982

Arthur Marwick, *British Society Since 1945*, Penguin, 1982

James McMillan, *The Way it Changed*, Life in Britain 1951-1975, William Kimber and Co Ltd, 1987

John Peacock, *Fashion Sketchbook 1920-1960*, Thames and Hudson, 1977

Dr John Pimlott, *South and Central America, Conflict in the 20th Century*, Aladdin Books, 1987

John Roy and James Hagerty, *The Twentieth-Century World*, Hutchinson, 1986

Valerie Schloredt and Pam Brown, *Martin Luther King*, Exley, 1988

Michael Scott-Baumann, *Links: Twentieth Century World History, Conflict in the Middle East*, Edward Arnold, 1987

Yesterday, A Photographic Album of Daily Life in Britain 1953-1970, J.M. Dent & Sons Ltd, 1982

Acknowledgments

The Author and Publisher would like to thank the following for permission to reproduce illustrations; Associated Newspapers (page 21); Barnabys Picture Library (pages 22, 40, 54); Bettman Newsphotos (pages 13, 36-7); *Evening Standard* (page 32); The BBC Hulton Picture Library (pages 4, 8, 11, 24-7, 35, 42-5, 52, 55, 57-8, 63, 65); Keystone Collection (frontispiece and pages 5, 9, 10, 14, 16, 41, 44, 56, 61-2); Popperfoto (pages 3-4, 6-7, 15, 18-19, 21, 28-9, 31-2, 39, 49-50, 59); The Tate Gallery (page 64); and The Victoria and Albert Museum (page 34).

Index